THE DAY MARTIN LUTHER KING, JR., WAS SHOT

A Photo History of the Civil Rights Movement

Acknowledgements

I am grateful to Kathy Benson for her help

Dedication

To Pat and Fred

Book and Cover Design by Georgia Morrissey

Photo Research by Lisa Crawley

Front Cover: Bottom Left: Crispus Attucks, a runaway slave, is shot down by British soldiers during the Boston Massacre of 1770. (WPA/National Archives) Top Right: Dr. Martin Luther King, Jr., in the sanctuary of the Ebenezer Baptist Church, Atlanta, Georgia. (©1983 Flip Schulke/Black Star) Center: National Guardsmen escort the Little Rock Nine into Central High School, September 25, 1957. (Wide World) Bottom Right: A crowd of 200,000 gathers at the Lincoln Memorial for the March on Washington, August 28, 1963. (Wide World) Back Cover: Harriet Tubman (far left) with a group of ex-slaves she helped deliver to freedom through the Underground Railroad. (Courtesy of the Sophia Smith Collection, Smith College)

ISBN 0-590-43661-9
Copyright © 1992 by James Haskins.
All rights reserved. Published by Scholastic Inc.

12 11   0 1 2/0
Printed in the U.S.A.   40
First Scholastic printing, January 1992

THE DAY MARTIN LUTHER KING, JR., WAS SHOT

A Photo History of the Civil Rights Movement

by Jim Haskins

SCHOLASTIC INC.

New York   Toronto   London   Auckland   Sydney

TABLE OF CONTENTS

End of an Era

On Thursday, April 4, 1968, just after six o'clock in the evening, the Reverend Martin Luther King, Jr., stepped out onto the balcony in front of his room on the second floor of the Lorraine Motel in Memphis, Tennessee. He was late for a dinner he had promised to attend.

He often ran behind schedule, but lately he had seemed to be more deliberate in his movements. Some people who were close to him felt that he was preparing himself for the possibility that his life might be cut short.

The evening before, he had delivered an unusual speech at the Mason Street Temple in Memphis. The meeting was to prepare striking black sanitation workers and their supporters for a march the following day. Dr. King talked of threats on his life. Then he paused. He seemed to realize that he was making the crowd nervous. He started again on a positive note:

"But it really doesn't matter to me now," he said. "Because I've been to the *mountaintop*! Like anybody I would like to live . . . a long life. . . . But I'm

Pictured left to right: Hosea Williams, Jesse Jackson, Dr. King, and Ralph Abernathy, on the balcony of the Lorraine Motel the day before Dr. King's assassination.

"All the News That's Fit to Print"

The New York Times

LATE CITY EDITION

Weather: Clearing today, turning cold tonight. Fair, cool tomorrow. Temp. range: today 62-44; Thurs. 73-52. Full U.S. report on Page 92.

VOL. CXVII . No. 40,249

NEW YORK, FRIDAY, APRIL 5, 1968

10 CENTS

MARTIN LUTHER KING IS SLAIN IN MEMPHIS; A WHITE IS SUSPECTED; JOHNSON URGES CALM

JOHNSON DELAYS TRIP TO HAWAII; MAY LEAVE TODAY

President Spends a Hectic Day Here and in Capital —Sees Thant at the U.N.

By MAX FRANKEL
Special to The New York Times

WASHINGTON, April 4 — President Johnson postponed his trip to Hawaii at least until tomorrow after he heard of the death of the Rev. Dr. Martin Luther King Jr. tonight.

The news, which visibly shocked the President, came at the end of one of the most extraordinary days in perhaps the most extraordinary week of his Administration.

Mr. Johnson was to have flown from Washington at about midnight for a weekend of strategy conferences with his military and diplomatic leaders stationed in South Vietnam. On the way, he had planned a breakfast meeting in California with former President Dwight D. Eisenhower.

Instead, the President telephoned Mrs. King in Atlanta, made a brief appeal for calm on television and went to his office to follow the reports of unrest and disturbance given him periodically by Attorney General Ramsey Clark.

Cancels Dinner Appearance

Mr. Johnson also canceled an appearance before a Democratic party fund-raising dinner here—the final event of a hectic schedule that became ever more hectic as the day unfolded.

The President began the day by making final arrangements for the Hawaii meeting. It had been tentatively planned before his order Sunday to curtail the bombing of North Vietnam and the news yesterday that Hanoi was interested in establishing direct contact.

[The new United States peace moves are producing a quiet but bitter reaction in the South Vietnamese Government that is causing increasing concern among United States officials in Saigon. Page 14.]

But the diplomatic development, though not the principal subject of the Honolulu meetings, added special weight to his conversations with Gen. Wiliam C. Westmoreland, the American commander in South Vietnam, and other officials.

Mr. Johnson was careful not to arouse false hopes of peace, but he appeared encouraged and in buoyant spirt as he decided before noon to fly first to New York to attend the investiture of the Most Rev. Terence J. Cooke as Archbishop of New York.

Then, while in New York,

Continued on Page 12, Column 1

Hanoi Charges U.S. Raid Far North of 20th Parallel

By EVERT CLARK
Special to The New York Times

WASHINGTON, April 4 — North Vietnam charged in a broadcast today that United States planes had bombed a "populated area" in northwestern Vietnam far north of the 20th parallel. The Defense Department said it knew of no such raid but was investigating.

President Johnson has ordered that there be no attacks on North Vietnam north of the 20th Parallel as a step toward de-escalating the war.

[In South Vietnam, United States marines beat off an attack by about 400 North Vietnamese soldiers charging up a hill near Khesanh, killing 93, The Associated Press reported. Meanwhile, an American relief column was nearing the besieged base. Page 15.]

The Hanoi radio, in a broadcast monitored and translated here, said three waves of United States planes dropped more than 50 bombs on a "populated area" about 30 miles west of Laichau, capital of Laichau Province, this morning.

The nearest village to that

Continued on Page 15, Column 1

The New York Times April 5, 1968

Hanoi said that area near Laichau (cross) was target.

HUMPHREY HINTS HE'LL ENTER RACE

Tells Unionists in Pittsburgh He Will Act Soon—Abel and Wirtz Back Him

By ROY REED
Special to The New York Times

PITTSBURGH, April 4—Two thousand labor representatives, including the head of the United Steel Workers union, clamorously urged Vice President Humphrey today to run for President.

The Vice President left little doubt that he would oblige them, but he indicated that he would wait until President Johnson returned from his Hawaii conference before making an announcement.

"I know what your request is, and I know what your thoughts are," he told the delegates to the Pennsylvania A.F.L.-C.I.O. convention. "I am most grateful. I am not one to walk away from a decision, and a decision will come in due time."

But nothing he does should interfere with President Johnson's peace mission, he said.

Several other political leaders urged Mr. Humphrey today to enter the race for the Democratic Presidential nomination. The most prominent among them was Secretary of Labor W. Willard Wirtz, who was addressing a union convention at Miami Beach.

I. W. Abel, president of the steelworkers Union, rose as Mr.

Continued on Page 32, Column 1

Johnson Shuns Role Of '68 'Lame Duck,' Kennedy Was Told

By JOHN HERBERS
Special to The New York Times

WASHINGTON, April 4—In his meeting with Senator Robert F. Kennedy yesterday President Johnson said he would remain out of the political fight this year because he did not believe it was appropriate for a "lame duck" President to try to pick his successor.

This and other details of the Johnson-Kennedy meeting were learned today from knowledgeable sources.

The meeting, which Senator Kennedy had requested in the interest of "national unity," was described as an extraordinarily friendly one, with both the Senator and the President speaking in a conciliatory manner.

President Johnson was pictured as the "elder statesman" of the party who had decided to remain aloof from this year's scramble for the Presidency in an effort to keep the party as strong as possible and retain his own dignity and effectiveness as President.

At one point, it was reported, the President said he did not want to make a spectacle of himself as a lame duck President attempting to dictate to the party who should be nominated at the national convention.

In this regard, he pointed out that in 1956 former President Harry S. Truman went to the

Continued on Page 31, Column 4

DISMAY IN NATION

Negroes Urge Others to Carry on Spirit of Nonviolence

By LAWRENCE VAN GELDER

Dismay, shame, anger and foreboding marked the nation's reaction last night to the Rev. Dr. Martin Luther King Jr.'s murder.

From the high offices of state to the man in the street, news of the moderate civil rights leader's violent death in Memphis yesterday drew, for the most part, stunned and sober statements.

Most major Negro organizations and Negro leaders, lamenting Dr. King's death, expressed hope that it serve as a spur to others to carry on in his spirit of nonviolence. But some Negro militants responded with bitterness and anger.

Roy Wilkins, executive director of the National Association for the Advancement of Colored People, said his organization was "shocked and deeply grieved by the dastardly murder of Dr. Martin Luther King."

"His murderer or murderers must be promptly apprehended and brought to justice," Mr. Wilkins said.

'A Man of Peace'

"Dr. King was a symbol of the nonviolent civil rights protest movement. He was a man of peace, of dedication, of great courage. His senseless assassination solves nothing. It will not stay the civil rights movement; it will instead spur it to greater activity."

Whitney M. Young Jr., executive director of the National Urban League, said:

"We are unspeakably shocked by the murder of Martin Luther King, one of the greatest leaders of our time. This is a bitter reflection on America. We fear for our country.

"The only possible answer now is for the nation to act immediately on what Dr. King has been fighting for—passage of the civil rights and antipoverty bills and a true and just equality for all men. Those of us who have remained loyal to his concept of nonviolence have been dealt a mortal blow."

Mayor Richard G. Hatcher of Gary, Ind., a Negro, termed the death of Dr. King "every man's loss."

"Men who care for humankind and struggle for its salvation through reason and faith have lost a leader of monumental stature," he said. "A man of his magnitude will not soon pass this way again."

At his home in Stamford, Conn., the former baseball star Jackie Robinson called the

Continued on Page 26, Column 1

PRESIDENT'S PLEA

On TV, He Deplores 'Brutal' Murder of Negro Leader

Statements by Johnson and Humphrey are on Page 24.

Special to The New York Times

WASHINGTON, April 4— President Johnson deplored tonight in a brief television address to the nation the "brutal slaying" of the Rev. Dr. Martin Luther King Jr.

He asked "every citizen to reject the blind violence that has struck Dr. King, who lived by nonviolence."

Mr. Johnson said he was postponing his scheduled departure tonight for a Honolulu conference on Vietnam and that instead he would leave tomorrow.

The President spoke from the White House. At the Washington Hilton Hotel, where Democratic members of Congress had gathered to honor the President and the Vice President, Mr. Humphrey, his voice strained with emotion, said:

"Martin Luther King stands with our other American martyrs in the cause of freedom and justice. His death is a terrible tragedy."

The dinner was canceled 10 to 15 minutes after the Vice President spoke. Mr. Johnson, who was scheduled to appear at the dinner, canceled his plans to attend.

F.B.I. Inquiry Ordered

Attorney General Ramsey Clark ordered an immediate inquiry by the Federal Bureau of Investigation into the shooting of Dr. King in Memphis.

He said the purpose of the investigation would be to determine whether any Federal law had been violated.

One provision of the law that could be invoked makes it a crime to engage in a conspiracy to deprive a person of his civil rights.

In addition to F.B.I. agents, Department of Justice civil rights representatives were on the scene in Memphis and were in touch with the Attorney General.

Military sources said that no National Guard units had yet been Federalized and no Regular Army troops had been alerted yet for possible movement to cities where violence had broken out.

National Guard troops, such as the 4,000 men who have been called into Memphis, remain under state control until the responsible Governor requests help and the President

Continued on Page 24, Column 7

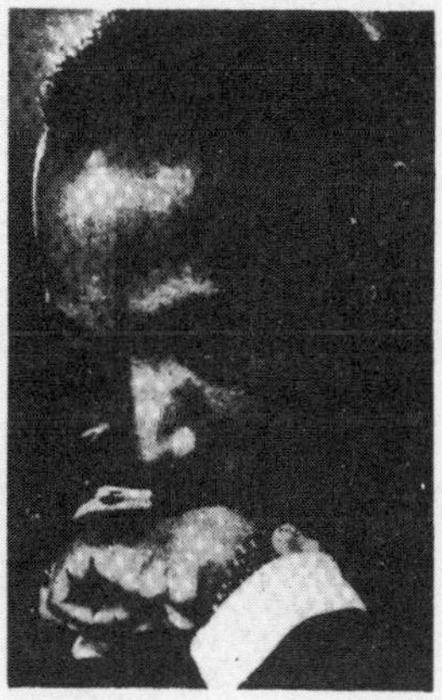

Associated Press

THE REV. DR. MARTIN LUTHER KING Jr.

Scattered Violence Occurs In Harlem and Brooklyn

12 Are Arrested Here

By THOMAS A. JOHNSON

Sporadic violence erupted in Harlem and Brooklyn's Bedford-Stuyvesant section last night after news of Dr. Martin Luther King's assassination spread in the two predominantly Negro communities.

Mayor Lindsay, who went to Harlem in an effort to quiet the outbreaks, was caught in the midst of an unruly crowd and had to be hustled into a limousine by bodyguards.

Police reinforcements, including elements of the riot-trained Tactical Patrol Force, were rushed into both communities.

Two arrests were reported in Brooklyn and 10 in Harlem. A television crewman was said to have been injured by flying glass.

There were numerous instances of rock-throwing, looting and arson reported both in Brooklyn and in Harlem, starting around 11 P.M. and continuing early today.

Gangs of youth in both areas were reported roaming through the streets, now and then taunting policemen and firemen on duty.

The police fired several volleys of shots in the air to disperse crowds along Brooklyn's Fulton Street and Harlem's

Continued on Page 26, Column 2

Widespread Disorders

Disorders broke out in scattered parts of the nation last night after the slaying of the Rev. Dr. Martin Luther King Jr. The National Guard was called out or alerted in several cities.

In Washington, scattered but persistent looting and vandalism erupted, led for a time by Stokely Carmichael, former head of the Student Nonviolent Coordinating Commitee. All available policemen were being called to duty.

About 4,000 Tennessee National Guardsmen were ordered to duty in Nashville because of disorders.

In North Carolina, Gov. Dan K. Moore alerted the Guard in Greensboro at the request of Mayor Carson Bain. State Highway patrolmen were dispatched to Raleigh.

There were riotous outbursts

Continued on Page 26, Column 5

GUARD CALLED OUT

Curfew Is Ordered in Memphis, but Fires and Looting Erupt

By EARL CALDWELL
Special to The New York Times

MEMPHIS, Friday, April 5— The Rev. Dr. Martin Luther King Jr., who preached nonviolence and racial brotherhood, was fatally shot here last night by a distant gunman who then raced away and escaped.

Four thousand National Guard troops were ordered into Memphis by Gov. Buford Ellington after the 39-year-old Nobel Prize-winning civil rights leader died.

A curfew was imposed on the shocked city of 550,000 inhabitants, 40 per cent of whom are Negro.

But the police said the tragedy had been followed by incidents that included sporadic shooting, fires, bricks and bottles thrown at policemen, and looting that started in Negro districts and then spread over the city.

White Car Sought

Police Director Frank Holloman said the assassin might have been a white man who was "50 to 100 yards away in a flophouse."

Chief of Detectives W. P. Huston said a late model white Mustang was believed to have been the killer's getaway car. Its occupant was described as a bareheaded white man in his 30's, wearing a black suit and black tie.

The detective chief said the police had chased two cars near the motel where Dr. King was shot and had halted one that had two out-of-town men as occupants. The men were questioned but seemed to have nothing to do with the killing, he said.

Rifle Found Nearby

A high-powered 30.06-caliber rifle was found about a block from the scene of the shooting, on South Main Street. "We think it's the gun," Chief Huston said, reporting it would be turned over to the Federal Bureau of Investigation.

Dr. King was shot while he leaned over a second-floor railing outside his room at the Lorraine Motel. He was chatting with two friends just before starting for dinner.

One of the friends was a musician, and Dr. King had just asked him to play a Negro spiritual, "Precious Lord, Take My Hand," at a rally that was to have been held two hours later in support of striking Memphis sanitationmen.

Paul Hess, assistant adminis-

Continued on Page 24, Column 1

Archbishop Cooke Installed; President Looks On

By EDWARD B. FISKE

The Most Rev. Terence J. Cooke was installed as the seventh Roman Catholic Archbishop of New York yesterday in a historic pageant attended by the President of the United States and highlighted by prayers for the success of his peace efforts in Vietnam.

"Let us pray with all our hearts that God will inspire our President," the 47-year-old Archbishop said in his homily at St. Patrick's Cathedral.

"In the last few days, we have all admired his heroic efforts in the search for peace in Vietnam. We ask God to bless his efforts with success. May God inspire not only our President, but also other leaders and the leaders of all nations of the world to find a way to peace."

Then the Archbishop, speaking from a white marble pulpit and surrounded by a blaze of purple, gold and scarlet robes, addressed himself directly to Mr. Johnson, who sat below him in a front pew.

The President, sitting with his hands clasped and his legs crossed, listened with obvious intensity to the Archbishop's words.

"Mr. President," he said, "our hearts, our hopes, our continued prayers go with you."

Mr. Johnson, accompanied by his daughter, Mrs. Patrick J. Nugent, led a festive congregation of about 5,000 cardinals, bishops, priests, laymen, nuns, civic leaders

Continued on Page 38, Column 1

The New York Times (by Neal Boenzi)

President Johnson and his daughter, Mrs. Patrick J. Nugent, right, listening during yesterday's ceremonies. At left are Mrs. John F. Kennedy and Lieut. Gov. Malcolm Wilson. Security personnel are in the row between them.

Archbishop Luigi Raimondi, Apostolic Delegate to the U.S., speaking after Archbishop Terence J. Cooke was enthroned

Mourners line Atlanta's streets to pay their last respects to Dr. King, whose coffin is on a mule-drawn cart.

not *concerned* about that now. . . . I've *seen* the Promised Land! I may not get there with you, but I want you to know, tonight, that we as a people will get to the Promised Land."

The next night, the Reverends Andrew Young and Jesse Jackson were waiting for Dr. King in the parking lot below. The Reverend Ralph David Abernathy, Dr. King's assistant, was trying to get Dr. King to hurry up. From below Reverend Jackson said, "Oh, Doc—" Dr. King bent forward to look over the balcony railing.

Just then a crack split the air, and Dr. King fell to the floor of the balcony. The bullet had hit him with such force that it had knocked him flat on his back. Abernathy rushed to his friend. All

around the courtyard people stood screaming and moaning. Someone called for an ambulance. Someone else called the police. A local radio station cut into its regular programming with a special bulletin: Dr. Martin Luther King, Jr., had been shot.

At St. Joseph's Hospital in Memphis, doctors worked desperately over the unconscious King. But soon they realized it was useless. The bullet had cut through his spinal cord. He was declared officially dead at 7:05 PM. He had not yet reached his fortieth birthday.

All over the nation, all over the world, people were in shock. They cried. They sat glued to their televisions. Others did not pay much attention. And for others, the news was cause for rejoicing. They were certain that King's death would bring about an end to the civil rights movement.

Dr. King's murderer, James Earl Ray, was caught on June 8. He was later tried and convicted of King's assassination and sentenced to ninety-nine years in prison. He remains in prison as of this writing.

With the death of Dr. King, the resounding voice that had called for love and understanding between the races was stilled. While his death has been called the end of the civil rights era, he at least lived to see what the civil rights movement could accomplish. He could proudly look back on a history of 350 years and know that blacks had never given up the long struggle to be equal citizens under the law.

A veiled Coretta Scott King looks ahead during her husband's funeral service.

James Earl Ray is led to prison after receiving a 99-year jail sentence for the murder of Dr. Martin Luther King, Jr.

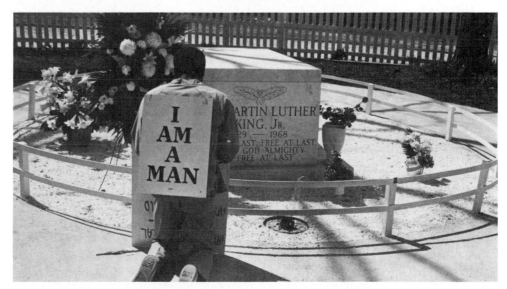

A striking sanitation worker kneels before the gravesite of Dr. Martin Luther King, Jr.

The Earliest Fighters for Freedom

From the beginning, from the time of the slave trade, blacks have fought for their rights. Many blacks resisted enslavement and were willing to die rather than give up their freedom.

Most Africans were captured and taken to the West Coast of Africa to be sold to the captains of slaveships. They were then taken out to the ships in long boats. So many slaves jumped overboard and drowned that the captains ordered them chained together. Even so, whole groups of chained-together slaves managed to jump into the tossing waves.

On board the ships, many slaves refused to eat, preferring to starve to death

Chained African villagers are led to the coast to be sold to slave traders.

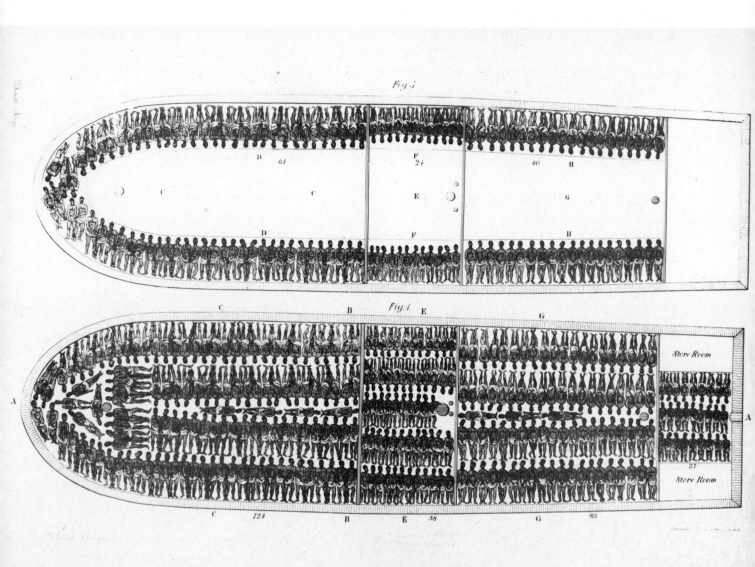

As these diagrams illustrate, enslaved Africans crossed the Atlantic Ocean lying pressed together in crowded ships' holds.

rather than meet the unknown fate that awaited them at the end of their journey.

Other slaves committed suicide by throwing themselves overboard, or slitting their own throats, or hanging themselves. And some died for no apparent reason. Slaveship doctors called it "fixed melancholy." We would call it dying of a broken heart.

There are also records of hundreds of mutinies aboard the slaveships.

What makes this record surprising is that in most cases the groups of slaves who mutinied did not even speak the same language. But the slaves found ways to communicate with one another anyway, often through music.

On deck, they often danced to drumming sounds made on the bottom of a tub or tin kettle. Slaveship captains did not realize it, but the drum sounds were a kind of code the slaves used to send signals to one another.

Most shipboard slave revolts took place while the ships were still in sight of the African coast. But at least 150 recorded mutinies took place far out at sea. And in several cases, the slaves managed to get back to Africa.

The most famous slave revolt aboard a ship occurred in 1839 on the *Amistad*, a Spanish slaveship bound for Cuba.

A portrait of Joseph Cinque, a Mendi chieftain and leader of the Amistad *revolt.*

Led by Joseph Cinque, the son of an African king, fifty-three Africans seized the ship and ordered a handful of sailors to head back to Africa. The crewmen, however, tricked the Africans and headed instead for the coast of New England. Off the coast of Long Island, Joseph Cinque and his men were captured.

By 1839 the Atlantic slave trade had been outlawed in the United States.

Former president John Quincy Adams, who volunteered to represent the slaves, argued that they should be allowed to go back to Africa. Spain argued that they belonged to Spain. The case went all the way to the United States Supreme Court, which ruled that the slaves should be returned to Africa.

The trial of the Amistad *captives before the United States Supreme Court.*

Former President John Quincy Adams argued the Amistad *case before the U.S. Supreme Court.*

An advertisement for the sale of slaves in New Orleans.

Slave Resistance in North America

A slave family stands on an auction block to be sold to the highest bidder.

Slave resistance did not end after the slaves arrived on the shores of North America. There are records of slave escapes and revolts on the plantations of the South and even in the cities of the North.

In 1739, in Stono, South Carolina, about two dozen slaves broke into a store and armed themselves with muskets, powder, and shot. They then headed south. Along the way, they were joined by about one hundred other blacks shouting "Liberty!"

About ten miles from where they started, the band of blacks met up with a band of armed whites. In the shoot-out that followed, most of the blacks were killed.

Although the insurrection was put down, the Stono Rebellion put fear into the hearts of whites throughout the British colonies.

As time went on, slaves who spoke different languages learned to communicate with each other using a form of broken English called "pidgin." But Southern plantation slaves also used music to communicate with each other. They made drums and used the drum sounds as calls to revolt.

When it finally became clear to slave masters that the drums were being used in this way, they outlawed drums. But that did not stop the slaves. They kept the drumbeat alive by using their feet. The sounds they were able to make with their heels were so much like drum sounds that only the keenest ear could tell the difference.

After a time, most slaves converted to Christianity, the religion of their masters. They responded to the message that there was a heaven where they would be freed of their heavy burdens on earth. But they also used the new religion to gain freedom in this world.

Again, one way was through music. Christian slaves developed songs called spirituals. Also called sorrow songs, they expressed the suffering of the slaves and their longing for the peaceful kingdom of heaven. But these songs were also a way to send secret signals to each other.

African drummers and dancers gathered at Congo Square in New Orleans.

"O Freedom," a popular Negro spiritual sung by blacks during slavery.

Slave insurrections were often led by slave preachers. A planned revolt in Camden, South Carolina, in 1816 was led by a slave preacher. In 1839, in Mississippi, there were rumors of a revolt planned by traveling preachers.

In 1822 in Charleston, South Carolina, Denmark Vesey, a carpenter who had bought his freedom in 1800, plotted to seize the city. But someone informed the police, and Vesey and other leaders of the plot were arrested and executed.

Nine years later, in 1831, a slave named Nat Turner led a revolt in Southampton, Virginia. A deeply religious man, who was a country preacher, he had a vision one night that it was his duty to end slavery. The revolt, however, was put down and he was hung.

Nat Turner, preacher and leader of one of America's most famous slave revolts, is discovered in Virginia's Dismal Swamp in 1831.

Freedom for the Colonies

An escaped slave named Crispus Attucks was one of the first to die in the revolutionary cause. It was in Boston in the fall of 1770. British troops were in the city to enforce the laws passed by King George of England. One night a group of citizens got into a scuffle with some soldiers. When the redcoats fired on the crowd, Attucks was the first to fall.

Six years later, both free blacks and slaves fought in the Revolutionary War. There were two all-black units in the Continental Army, one from Massachusetts and one from Rhode Island, as well as a third that came from Haiti with the French allies of the colonies.

Many of the privately owned ships that fought in the revolutionary cause had black crewmen. James Forten was among them. Born free in Philadelphia in 1766, he enlisted at the age of fifteen as a powder boy on the privateer *Royal Louis*. When his ship was captured by a British frigate, Forten was taken prisoner. After seven months on a prison ship, he was released in a general exchange of prisoners.

All of these black veterans of the Revolutionary War fought for a country that did not even recognize them as citizens.

Meanwhile, blacks, slave and free, responded to the talk of independence

Crispus Attucks, a runaway slave, is shot down by British soldiers during the Boston Massacre of 1770.

Black Revolutionary War soldiers fight against an attack from British troops.

A portrait of James Forten, a freedman, abolitionist, and ship captain, who served during the American Revolution.

and calls for freedom by calling for their own freedom.

In the colony of Massachusetts, in the years 1773 and 1774, slaves, including "members of the Church of Christ," presented several petitions and letters to the colonial authorities asking that slavery be ended in the colony. "We have no Property! We have no Wives! No Children! We have no City! No Country!" cried one petition to Governor Hutchinson.

The Declaration of Independence of 1776, however, contained not one word about slaves or slavery. Slaves in several New England states filed more petitions asking to be given the same rights as the document had declared for other people. But their petitions went unanswered.

The African American Church

Absalom Jones, early church leader in Philadelphia and co-founder of the Free African Society (the first black self-help organization).

Richard Allen, bishop and founder of the Bethel African Methodist Episcopal Church in Philadelphia, PA.

Peter Williams, sexton of the John Street Methodist Episcopal Church of New York City, and founder of the African Methodist Episcopal Zion Church also of New York City.

The time of the American Revolution was also the time when the African American church was born. It was a way that black Americans could assert their own independence, as well as organize to push for their own freedom.

The first black Baptist church in America arose among slaves at Silver Bluff, South Carolina, between 1773 and 1775. David George, founder of that church, was a runaway slave who had hidden out with the Creek Indians and worked for a time as a servant to Creek Chief Blue Salt.

A little more than ten years later, Richard Allen and Absalom Jones, both of whom had been born in slavery but had purchased their freedom, decided to organize the blacks of Philadelphia. In the spring of 1787, they founded the Free African Society, devoted to black progress. It was the first such organization not only in America, but in all of the Western world.

About six months after they had formed the Free African Society, they were told they could not pray at the white St. George's Episcopal Church. Allen then formed his own church and called it the African Methodist Church.

In New York City, two black men named Peter Williams and James Varick broke away from the white John Street Church. On July 30, 1800, they laid the cornerstone for their own church, called Zion. In 1816 the Zion Church and other offshoots of Richard Allen's African Methodist Episcopal congregation met in Philadelphia to launch the first completely independent black church in the United States, the African Methodist Episcopal Zion Church. Allen was elected its first bishop.

During the Revolution, Prince Hall founded a black branch of the Masons, an international secret society with roots in the stone workers' guilds of the Middle Ages. In 1797, Richard Allen, Absalom Jones, the Revolutionary War veteran James Forten, and others formed a black Masonic Lodge for Pennsylvania. Hall traveled to Philadelphia to install the officers of the new lodge.

Philadelphia's African Episcopal Church of St. Thomas (circa 1829).

Prince Hall, a Revolutionary War soldier who later founded the first black masonic lodge in the United States.

The Abolitionist Movement

From the beginning, there were some free people, white and black, in North America who did not believe in slavery and felt it should be ended. They presented petitions, wrote articles, and gave speeches. But a strong, organized, militant movement to abolish slavery did not begin in the United States until the late 1820s.

Free blacks led the way. In 1827 the first black newspaper, *Freedom's Journal,* was published for the first time in New York City by John B. Russwurm and Samuel E. Cornish. Cornish was a black Presbyterian minister and Russwurm was the first black college graduate (Bowdoin College in Brunswick, Maine, 1826).

Around the same time, David Walker, born free in Wilmington, North Carolina, decided that he could not stay in that slaveholding community any longer. "If I remain in this bloody land," he said, "I will not live long." He moved to Boston, and in 1829 he published *Walker's Appeal,* a pamphlet that urged slaves to "Kill or be killed."

In 1831 a white man named William Lloyd Garrison published the first issue of his abolitionist newspaper, *Liberator.* Two years later, he joined with James Forten, and other blacks and whites in Philadelphia, to found the American Anti-Slavery Society.

Two of the most famous African-American abolitionists were Frederick

John B. Russwurm, co-founder of Freedom's Journal, *the first abolitionist newspaper by African Americans.*

William Lloyd Garrison, leading abolitionist and publisher of the anti-slavery newspaper, the Liberator.

One of the most important anti-slavery newspapers of its time, the Liberator was published in Boston for 31 years.

Pennsylvania Hall, headquarters of the Abolition Society in Philadelphia, was burned by demonstrators in 1838.

Sojourner Truth, born a slave in New York, later gained her freedom and became a prominent abolitionist and activist for many reform causes, including women's rights.

Harriet Beecher Stowe, famous author of Uncle Tom's Cabin.

Frederick Douglass, the foremost black abolitionist of his time, was a popular speaker on the anti-slavery lecture circuit and editor of the North Star.

Douglass and Sojourner Truth. Douglass was born a slave in Baltimore, Maryland. In 1838, at the age of twenty-one, he escaped to New York. Three years after that, he spoke at an abolitionists' meeting for the first time, telling his audience about his life as a slave. He was such a good speaker that he was soon spending most of his time giving lectures at anti-slavery meetings. He even traveled to England and Ireland, where people who heard him speak gave money to support the abolition movement. In 1847 he founded his own abolitionist newspaper, *North Star,* in Rochester, New York. From that time until slavery was abolished, he worked tirelessly to bring about its end.

Sojourner Truth was also born a slave, in upstate New York. When New York abolished slavery in 1827, she became free. But she understood that there were millions of slaves who were not so lucky. She made her way to New York City, gave up her birth name, Isabella, for a new name and joined the abolition movement. Her new name, Sojourner Truth, described what she spent the rest of her life doing: She sojourned, or traveled about, talking about the evils of slavery. Deeply religious, she believed that she was on a mission for God.

For nearly forty years, the abolitionists tried to bring about the end of slavery through speeches, newspapers and pamphlets, and conventions. They were successful in the North, where each state abolished slavery at last. But they were not successful in the South, where slavery was as deeply rooted as ever. Tired of all the talking, people like John Brown and Harriet Tubman put the words into action.

The Underground Railroad

Harriet Tubman was born a slave in Maryland and escaped when she was about twenty-eight. She later explained her reason for running away: "There was one or two things I had a *right* to, liberty or death; if I could not have one, I would have the other." Once she escaped to the North and freedom, she could have stayed there. But she chose instead to risk her life by going back to the South to help other slaves escape.

Harriet Tubman was the most famous "conductor" on the Underground Railroad. This was a route from the South

A young Harriet Tubman became the "Moses of her people" by leading over 300 slaves to freedom on the Underground Railroad.

Harriet Tubman (far left) with a group of ex-slaves she led to freedom.

Henry "Box" Brown was shipped to Underground Railroad agents in Philadelphia by traveling in a box with some biscuits.

to Canada and freedom. Its conductors were whites and blacks who helped the slaves get from one safe house or "depot" to another. Between 1848 and 1858, Tubman returned to the South nineteen times and brought out more than three hundred slaves. By 1852, rewards offered for her capture amounted to $40,000. But she was never caught.

John Brown was a white man and a devout Christian who, on October 16, 1859, led a group of twenty-two men,

John Brown is comforted by a child's kiss while he is led to the gallows.

seventeen of whom were white, including his own sons. Their target was the federal arsenal at Harpers Ferry, Virginia. They planned to use the weapons and ammunition they seized there to arm the slaves whom they would help to escape to the mountains. Left in the house was Brown's sixteen-year-old daughter and seventeen-year-old daughter-in-law, who were lookouts.

Brown and his group were successful in seizing the arsenal and in taking about sixty people hostage. But federal troops commanded by Colonel Robert E. Lee put down the assault on the arsenal. In the process, they killed ten men, among them two of Brown's sons. Five men escaped, and seven were captured, including John Brown, who was later hanged.

Neither the talk nor the action of the abolitionists ended slavery. And even free blacks had only second class legal status in most states, North as well as South. In 1857, two years before John Brown's raid on the Harpers Ferry arsenal, the U.S. Supreme Court ruled in the Dred Scott case that blacks, free or slave, were not United States citizens.

Ellen Craft, a runaway slave who escaped to the North by train, disguised as her husband's master.

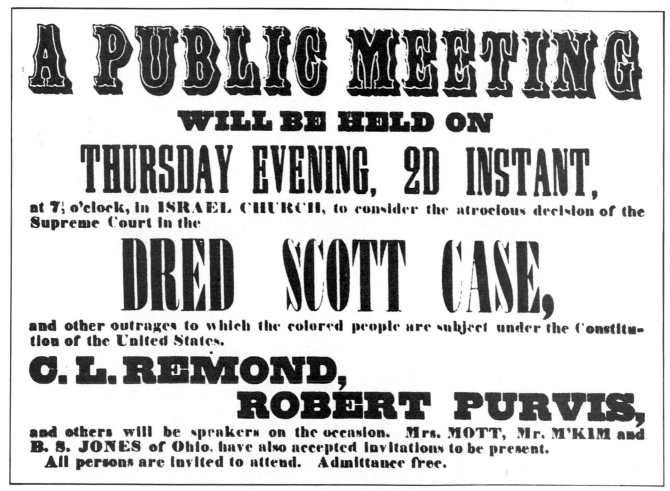

A PUBLIC MEETING

WILL BE HELD ON

THURSDAY EVENING, 2D INSTANT,

at 7½ o'clock, in ISRAEL CHURCH, to consider the atrocious decision of the Supreme Court in the

DRED SCOTT CASE,

and other outrages to which the colored people are subject under the Constitution of the United States.

C. L. REMOND,
ROBERT PURVIS,

and others will be speakers on the occasion. Mrs. MOTT, Mr. M'KIM and B. S. JONES of Ohio, have also accepted invitations to be present.
All persons are invited to attend.   Admittance free.

An announcement of a meeting headed by black abolitionists to discuss the famous Dred Scott case where the Supreme Court ruled slaveholders could not be deprived of their property in any part of the Union.

The War Between the States

President Abraham Lincoln's "Emancipation Proclamation" of January 1, 1863, which called for the freedom of those slaves residing in Confederate territory.

The Civil War did not begin because of slavery alone. The two regions of the nation also had economic and political disagreements. The main reason why the seven Confederate States seceded in 1861 was political: They believed in states' rights and refused to submit to federal control. The main reason why President Lincoln ordered federal troops to put down the southern insurrection was to maintain the Union.

President Lincoln's Emancipation Proclamation of 1863 was one more weapon to preserve the Union. It did not free all slaves, only those in the Confederate states. But slaves, free blacks, and white abolitionists rejoiced and did whatever they could to aid the Union side.

Southern slaves escaped in droves, seeking refuge with the Union forces. Many of those who could not reach the Union lines offered their own resistance. There were reports of slave plots to burn Confederate ships and of southern slaves acting as Union spies. It soon became clear that the Confederacy was fighting two enemies: the Union forces and "the enemy within," their own slaves.

Among the "enemy within" were hundreds of slave women who hid Union soldiers stranded behind Confederate lines and helped them to escape. These women also brought food to the Union prisoners of war. Slave men and women acted as spies for the Union.

The Confederacy pressed thousands of slaves into its cause. Skilled slaves served in combat roles, and whenever they could, they undermined their masters' cause. Robert Smalls, the slave pilot of the Confederate battleship *Planter*, fought for both sides during the war. On the night of May 13, 1863, the white captain and officers were ashore. Smalls and the other African American crewmen on board sailed the ship out

Robert Smalls, crew member of the Confederate gunboat the Planter, *who steered the vessel into Union territory.*

Commanding officer of the Massachusetts 54th Regiment, Colonel Robert Gould Shaw.

Peter Vogelsang, one of three black officers in the Massachusetts 54th Regiment.

A black civil war regiment, with rifles and sabers, stands at ease in front of an army barracks.

of Charleston harbor and surrendered it to the Union Navy. For the rest of the war, Smalls served the Union as captain of the *Planter*.

By 1862 there were some 50,000 black soldiers, slave and free, in the Union Army. They were paid less money than the white soldiers, they were not allowed to hold positions of command, and they faced greater danger if they were captured. But they clamored to get into the fighting.

By 1863 the white Union forces were depleted and President Lincoln had no choice but to allow more blacks to enlist. He admitted that without them, "we would be compelled to abandon the war in 3 weeks."

Approximately 179,000 black soldiers served in 166 all-black regiments in the Union Army. One out of every four Union sailors was black. They did not receive as much pay or equipment as white troops, but when it came to fighting, many black soldiers and sailors put aside their resentments toward unequal treatment and fought bravely. On July 18, 1864, the 54th Massachusetts made a charge against a heavily fortified Fort Wagner in Charleston, South Carolina. So many died or were wounded that the regiment was forced to retreat, but their heroism won them great admiration in the North.

The Congressional Medal of Honor was created during the Civil War to honor brave Union soldiers and sailors. Twenty-two blacks won that medal for their courage and fighting ability during the war. Many more deserved the honor

This Civil War portrait depicts the promises of freedom and education for blacks as Union troops take hold of Confederate territory.

During the New York City draft riots of 1863 a black man is lynched on Brooklyn's Clarkson Street.

A Union Army soldier pictured with his wife, 1865.

than received it, for in the course of the war 37,300 blacks were killed, a far greater percentage of casualties than the white troops suffered.

By early January 1865, Confederate General Robert E. Lee was so short of reinforcements that he recommended arming slaves. But it was a last act of desperation. The Union forces were prevailing on every front. At the end of the month, Congress passed the Thirteenth Amendment, which abolished slavery not just in the Confederate states but in all of the states. After ratification by the states, it became part of the Constitution in December.

Robert E. Lee surrendered on April 9, 1865. The Confederacy was crushed. African Americans rejoiced, but they recognized that their struggle was only beginning. Freedom meant little without legal rights. By May, mass meetings of blacks demanding equal rights and the vote were being held all over the South.

General Robert E. Lee, leader of the Confederate Army.

President Abraham Lincoln and son Tad stroll through a jubilant crowd in the fallen Confederate capital of Richmond, Virginia, April 1865.

Reconstruction

Those who attended the mass meetings believed they knew what should be done for the slaves. But many others, white and black—including the newly freed slaves, who were called freedmen—did not. A Pennsylvania congressman named Thaddeus Stevens suggested giving each slave forty acres of land and a mule. Congress approved this idea, and it actually began to be put into effect. But it did not last long and comparatively few freedmen ever received the promised land.

Educated blacks, most of whom were already free before the war ended, wanted the vote and the right to an equal education. But many former slaves in the South had no idea what freedom meant. They could not read or write or do simple figures. They had no land and no way to support themselves or their families. The federal government determined that something had to be done to help these freedmen.

President Lincoln wanted to help the former slaves gain full freedom. He also

Official city records citing the transfer of the remains of President Lincoln to his burial place in Springfield, Illinois.

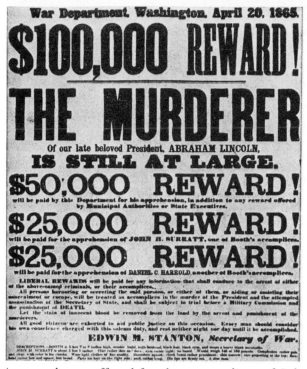

War Department, Washington, April 20, 1865.

$100,000 REWARD!

THE MURDERER

Of our late beloved President, ABRAHAM LINCOLN,

IS STILL AT LARGE.

$50,000 REWARD!

will be paid by this Department for his apprehension, in addition to any reward offered by Municipal Authorities or State Executives.

$25,000 REWARD!

will be paid for the apprehension of JOHN H. SURRATT, one of Booth's accomplices.

$25,000 REWARD!

will be paid for the apprehension of DANIEL C. HARROLD, another of Booth's accomplices.

LIBERAL REWARDS will be paid for any information that shall conduce to the arrest of either of the above-named criminals, or their accomplices.

All persons harboring or secreting the said persons, or either of them, or aiding or assisting their concealment or escape, will be treated as accomplices in the murder of the President and the attempted assassination of the Secretary of State, and shall be subject to trial before a Military Commission and the punishment of DEATH.

Let the stain of innocent blood be removed from the land by the arrest and punishment of the murderers.

All good citizens are exhorted to aid public justice on this occasion. Every man should consider his own conscience charged with this solemn duty, and rest neither night nor day until it be accomplished.

EDWIN M. STANTON, Secretary of War.

DESCRIPTIONS.—BOOTH is 5 feet 7 or 8 inches high, slender build, high forehead, black hair, black eyes, and wears a heavy black mustache. JOHN H. SURRATT is about 5 feet 9 inches. Hair rather thin and dark, eyes rather light; no beard. Would weigh 145 or 150 pounds. Complexion rather pale and clear, with color in his cheeks. Wore light clothes of fine quality. Shoulders square; cheek bones rather prominent; chin narrow; ears projecting at the top; forehead rather low and square, but broad. Parts his hair on the right side; neck rather long. His lips are firmly set. A slim man.

A reward was offered for the accomplices of John Wilkes Booth in the assassination of President Abraham Lincoln.

wanted to get the former Confederate states back into the Union as soon as possible. But he was assassinated by John Wilkes Booth on April 15, 1865, before he could put his plans into action.

No one mourned the death of Lincoln more than African Americans, for whom he had been the Great Emancipator. They feared that their hopes for equality were dashed. Vice President Andrew Johnson, who succeeded to the presidency on the death of Lincoln, tried to continue Lincoln's plan.

One part of the plan that Lincoln had lived to see enacted, and that Johnson continued to support, was the Freedmen's Bureau. Its purpose was to provide for the needs of the former slaves so that they could eventually become self-sufficient and to gain black political support for the Republican Party. The Freedman's Bureau brought medical help and food to the conquered South, and

not just to the freedmen but to poor whites, as well. The bureau set up schools and kept records of white violence against the freedmen. But it was poorly financed, its staff was not well trained, and there was much left undone for the four million freedmen who needed the bureau's help.

Meanwhile, white governments in the former Confederate states passed laws called Black Codes to restrict the rights and even the freedom of movement of the former slaves. Most of these laws were aimed at keeping the slaves working for white farmers on the plantations so that the South could rebuild its economy.

Angered at the actions of the defeated states, in 1866 Congress passed the Fourteenth Amendment to the Constitution (which was ratified in 1868). It made former slaves citizens of both the

This Harper's Weekly *illustration shows black men casting their ballots for the first time with the passage of the Fifteenth Amendment.*

A freedmen's school in Memphis, Tennessee, is burned during a riot.

A Thomas Nast cartoon depicts the rise of the Ku Klux Klan in the South during Reconstruction.

Passage of the Fifteenth Amendment was marked by celebrations nationwide.

United States and the state in which they lived and held that no state could pass any law that abridged their privileges. Congress also passed a Civil Rights Bill banning discrimination and segregation in schools, churches, hotels, and public transportation. The South responded by killing hundreds of freedmen in race riots across the region.

Led by men who wished to punish the South for its treatment of the freedmen and its refusal to obey the new Civil Rights law, Congress passed, in 1867, the first of a series of Reconstruction Acts. The former Confederate states were deprived of their right to govern themselves. The states were ordered to hold constitutional conventions and give freedmen the right to vote.

That same year, the Ku Klux Klan was organized in Nashville, Tennessee. A secret organization whose members hid their identities under white cloaks and hoods, the aim of the Klan was to use terror to put down the former slaves and their northern allies.

In 1870, the Fifteenth Amendment to the Constitution was ratified. It stated that the right to vote could not be denied because of "race, color, or previous condition of servitude."

During the brief time when the South was under Reconstruction, free blacks and freedmen enjoyed political rights that they had only dreamed about. In some states, like South Carolina, black delegates were in the majority at the constitutional convention. Pinckney Benton Stewart Pinchback, who was born free in Louisiana, served as acting governor of that state for a brief time. Ex-slave Blanche Kelso Bruce was elected to the U.S. House of Representatives from Mississippi.

The new state constitutions, crafted in large measure by blacks, were for-

Freedmen, both young and old, gather for their lessons at one of the many schools throughout the South set up by the Freedmen's Bureau.

Charlotte L. Forten Grimke, a native of Massachusetts, who established a school for the children of ex-slaves in the Sea Islands of South Carolina.

A Currier & Ives illustration of black elected officials who served in Congress at the state and national level during Reconstruction.

ward-looking. They abolished all forms of slavery and imprisonment for debt and authorized the vote for all men over the age of twenty-one. Black delegates were largely responsible for the establishment of a public school system open to all. In no case did black delegates authorize punishment for whites or try to dominate or deny whites any rights.

Most of the black delegates and legislators were more educated than their white counterparts, and most were sincere in their desire to create a government for the good of all. They worked for that goal in spite of violent white resistance that took the form of riots and lynchings, and they forced the federal government to send troops to the South again and again.

Congress continued to make laws that would ensure the civil rights of African Americans. The Civil Rights Act of 1875 stated that all persons were entitled to "full and equal enjoyment" of public places and services, and were to be allowed to serve on juries in all court systems in the country. It further provided that anyone found guilty of denying a person his civil rights could be punished.

But that was the last Reconstruction legislation enacted. Even though the former Confederate states openly disobeyed the new law, and all the other laws aimed at guaranteeing civil rights to African Americans, in 1877 the new president, Rutherford B. Hayes, ordered federal troops to leave the South.

Jim Crow

A black family in front of a cabin on a homestead claim near Guthrie, Oklahoma, 1889.

Reconstruction was over, and a new era of terror for southern blacks was about to begin. Southern states quickly passed restrictive laws. Southern blacks could see what lay ahead, and they left the South in droves. Some went North. Others headed for the American frontier and played a major part in taming it and shaping its future. They established black towns, bought farms, and built schools. They were every bit as important in the westward movement as the white pioneers.

For those African Americans who remained in the South, life became more and more grim. By 1887 the black officeholders had been voted out, and new, all-white southern legislatures had begun to pass a series of laws aimed at segregating, or separating blacks in every area of life. They were called Jim Crow laws, after a minstrel character, a white man who performed in blackface makeup. Beginning with laws that set up separate railroad cars for blacks and whites, the Jim Crow system eventually

Bill Pickett, one of the many black cowboys who made their home on the western trails.

covered every aspect of life, including local laws in some areas that prevented blacks and whites from playing checkers together in public or looking out the same factory window at the same time.

African Americans did not sit back and allow segregation to become law without a fight. Beginning in the early 1880s, they challenged the laws in court. The most famous challenge to segrega-

All Colored People

THAT WANT TO

GO TO KANSAS,

On September 5th, 1877,

Can do so for $5.00

IMMIGRATION.

WHEREAS, We, the colored people of Lexington, Ky,. knowing that there is an abundance of choice lands now belonging to the Government, have assembled ourselves together for the purpose of locating on said lands. Therefore,

BE IT RESOLVED, That we do now organize ourselves into a Colony, as follows:— Any person wishing to become a member of this Colony can do so by paying the sum of one dollar ($1.00), and this money is to be paid by the first of September, 1877, in instalments of twenty-five cents at a time, or otherwise as may be desired.

RESOLVED. That this Colony has agreed to consolidate itself with the Nicodemus Towns, Solomon Valley, Graham County, Kansas, and can only do so by entering the vacant lands now in their midst, which costs $5.00.

RESOLVED, That this Colony shall consist of seven officers—President, Vice-President, Secretary, Treasurer, and three Trustees. President—M. M. Bell; Vice-President —Isaac Talbott; Secretary—W. J. Niles; Treasurer—Daniel Clarke; Trustees—Jerry Lee, William Jones, and Abner Webster.

RESOLVED, That this Colony shall have from one to two hundred militia, more or less, as the case may require, to keep peace and order, and any member failing to pay in his dues, as aforesaid, or failing to comply with the above rules in any particular, will not be recognized or protected by the Colony.

This handbill of 1877 advertising a mass migration of blacks to Kansas was widely distributed throughout the South.

tion was brought by Homer Plessy, who brought suit against the Louisiana railroad company that forced him to sit in a Jim Crow car. Plessy's case, *Plessy v. Ferguson,* went all the way to the United States Supreme Court, where Plessy's attorneys argued that segregation violated the Fourteenth Amendment.

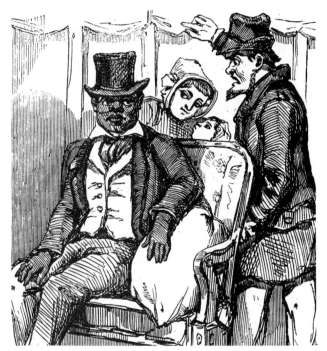

A black man is ordered off a city passenger car in Philadelphia, Pennsylvania, the only major Northern city where blacks were prohibited from riding passenger cars.

Mary Church Terrell, President of the National Association of Colored Women, which provided training and assistance to thousands of black families.

But on May 18, 1896, a majority of the justices decided that separate accommodations were constitutional as long as they were "equal." And that "separate but equal" decision opened the way for a system of legal segregation in the South that would last for more than sixty years.

Fight or Leave

Many southern blacks left the South, and its legal segregation, and moved North. Life was still hard for them there, but at least they had a better chance to get jobs, housing, and education that were denied them in the South.

But many more stayed. One black leader, Booker T. Washington, believed that it was best for blacks to learn to live under the southern legal system. Washington, born a slave in Virginia, founded Tuskegee Institute in 1881. Its

Portrait of a black family who migrated from the South to Chicago at the turn of the century.

George Washington Carver, seen here in his laboratory at Tuskegee Institute, 1939.

purpose was to train blacks in agricultural and mechanical trades so they could better themselves. But in a speech in Atlanta in 1895 he seemed to take pains to point out that blacks did not seek to become integrated into white society. "In all things that are purely social, we can be as separate as the fingers, yet as one hand in things essential to mutual progress."

Booker T. Washington, president and founder of Tuskegee Institute, urged blacks to unite with whites on issues related to Southern business and economy before fighting for equal civil and political rights.

W.E.B. Du Bois, sociologist and editor of the NAACP's official organ, the Crisis Magazine, *is pictured here in the New York office.*

Members of the Crisis Magazine *editorial staff in New York City included Harlem Renaissance writer Jessie Fauset (seated center) and W.E.B. Du Bois (standing).*

Some other black leaders criticized Washington. One was W.E.B. Du Bois, born free in Massachusetts, who had received a doctorate from Harvard University. He believed that blacks should fight for full equality. To further his beliefs, in 1910 he helped found the National Association for the Advancement of Colored People. The NAACP had influential and well-to-do whites as members, and it continues today to work for equal opportunity for blacks.

In 1911, one year after the NAACP was founded, the National Urban League was also founded by whites and blacks willing to work for racial equality.

Blacks and the Press

Thousands of New Yorkers march in the Silent Protest parade down Fifth Avenue, July 28, 1917, in response to a race riot in E. St. Louis, Illinois, which resulted in the deaths of 39 blacks.

Blacks in the North were learning that the press could be a powerful way to fight for equality. By 1900 there were some 150 black weekly newspapers. They were an important way to inform black people—and interested whites—of the issues that affected black people's lives.

These newspapers regularly reported on the horrible phenomenon of lynching. In the South, and occasionally in other parts of the country, the Ku Klux Klan or other mobs of whites, would hang blacks for little reason except that they were black. They would accuse their victims of "looking at a white

Ida Wells Barnett, a journalist and activist who launched a formal campaign against lynching in her newspaper The Memphis Free Speech.

Marcus Garvey, leader of the UNIA, the largest mass popular movement of blacks, advocated the establishment of an independent black nation on the African continent.

woman" or "acting uppity," and they would hang them.

Ida Wells Barnett was a black woman who fought against lynching by writing frequent articles in newspapers. She kept statistics showing that between 1890 and 1899, an average of two blacks per week were lynched in the South.

Faced with such statistics, more than a few blacks listened to leaders like Marcus Garvey, who said they should leave the United States altogether and go back to Africa.

Born in Jamaica, Garvey founded his Universal Negro Improvement Association (UNIA) there but moved his headquarters to the United States in 1916.

He believed that the best hope for blacks in the Western Hemisphere was to return to the homeland of their ancestors.

Garvey's organization did not appeal to educated blacks like W.E.B. Du Bois, but it did strike a chord in the hearts of many less educated black people. The UNIA held many mass meetings and parades and was well organized. But Garvey never saw his dream fulfilled. In December 1927 he was deported as an undesirable alien. He had never been able to attract the masses of black people. Most felt that, for better or for worse, America was their country. They preferred to stay and fight for their rights.

War and Peace

Blacks continued to fight for the United States in its various wars, including the Spanish-American War in 1898 and World War I in 1917. Segregationists kept trying to bar all nonwhites from military service, but black leaders urged their followers to join up nevertheless. It was the best way they knew to prove that blacks deserved equal citizenship rights.

All-black units, like the 369th Infantry from New York, distinguished themselves in World War I, but their fighting to "make the world safe for democracy" did not earn them any better treatment at home. Many whites were especially hostile to returning black veterans, fearing that they had become "uppity." In the summer of 1919, there were race riots in many northern cities and a notable increase in the number of lynchings in the South.

Things quieted down a bit during the prosperous 1920s. In Harlem, in New York City, an explosion of creativity on the part of black writers, artists, and musicians led to the Harlem Renaissance, a brief time when sophisticated whites supported African American cultural arts. But there was little integration. There were clubs in Harlem like the Cotton Club where all the waiters and performers were black but where blacks were not admitted as customers.

There was no comparable renaissance in the South, where life for blacks was as harsh as ever.

Black World War I soldiers taking a break.

A black serviceman saying good-bye to his wife before going off to war.

Young women of Harlem strolling down Seventh Avenue, in 1927.

W.C. Handy as a youth before he was known as the "Father of the Blues."

A young Langston Hughes, famous poet of the Harlem Renaissance.

The Depression and the New Deal

During the prosperous 1920s, many people got involved in the trading of securities on the New York Stock Exchange. They thought they were going to get rich when the stock prices went up. But suddenly the stock market crashed in October 1929 and the Great Depression soon followed.

Many businesses closed and many people lost their jobs. Blacks, always "last hired," were now "first fired." As a group, they suffered most during the Depression, for not only did they have to go through hard economic times, but also they still faced terrible discrimination.

In 1931 in Scottsboro, Alabama, a shocking case of unequal justice made headlines around the world. Nine black teenagers were accused of raping two white women on a freight train. Although there was no evidence against them, the nine suspects were convicted by an all-white jury and sentenced to death. NAACP lawyers went to Scottsboro to help the "Scottsboro Boys," and the lawyers were able to prevent the state of Alabama from executing them. But it was years before all of the young men were freed.

In 1937, Adam Clayton Powell, Jr., became minister of the Abyssinian Bap-

Members of the famous Scottsboro case in jail, awaiting their trial.

There's no way like the American Way

A billboard depicting the great American dream looms large above the heads of African Americans in line for relief supplies during the Depression.

Giving the black power salute during New York City's first Afro-American parade, are grand marshals Adam Clayton Powell, Jr., Harlem Congressman; and Shirley Chisholm, Brooklyn Congresswoman.

tist Church in New York when his father retired. A fiery preacher and a college graduate, he had a strong sense of how to organize blacks to protest their condition. He used his pulpit to call blacks in Harlem to action. He also used the press, writing a regular column in the black weekly *Amsterdam News*. He called on blacks in Harlem to boycott and protest against barriers that made New York as segregated as any southern city.

These attacks against segregation were successful, and in 1945 Powell used the base of support he had built to win a seat in Congress. In 1961, he was chair-

Civil rights activist and union leader, A. Philip Randolph, stands before the Lincoln Memorial during the March on Washington, August 28, 1963.

man of the Committee on Education and Labor and one of the most powerful politicians in America.

In 1937, the same year that Adam Clayton Powell, Jr., succeeded his father as minister of the Abyssinian Baptist Church, A. Philip Randoph won the right to form a union of black railroad porters. He had been fighting for twelve years to get his Brotherhood of Sleeping Car Porters recognized by the white labor organization, the American Federation of Labor. Before that time, the American labor movement had been all white. Randolph believed that racism was not so much a matter of color as a matter of economics. If blacks could make a decent living, they would be more accepted in white society. He also believed that if workers were to win lasting rights, black and white workers had to work together.

Meanwhile, the NAACP was quietly

A mother teaches her children the numbers and the alphabet in Louisiana, 1939.

Doctor S.A. Malloy
examining Louis
Graves and his
family, Farm
Security
Administration
borrowers, Caswell
County, N.C.,
Oct. 1940.

Mary McLeod
Bethune, founder of
Bethune-Cookman
College and director
of Franklin D.
Roosevelt's National
Youth Administration
program.

working against discrimination and segregation through the courts. During the
1930s, the organization won court rulings against laws and practices that
denied blacks basic rights. It was a slow
process, and the fight had to be carried
out on a case-by-case basis, but the
NAACP was making small cracks in the
wall of segregation.

During the Great Depression, President Franklin D. Roosevelt tried to help
blacks as well as whites with his New
Deal programs. He appointed a black
woman, Mary McLeod Bethune, as director of the Negro Affairs Division of
the National Youth Administration. Mrs.
Bethune worked all her life for greater
educational opportunities for blacks. She
founded Bethune College in Daytona
Beach, Florida.

President Roosevelt also began programs to give jobs to unemployed workers. Blacks were included in these programs. But it was the U.S. entry into
World War II that really lifted the United
States out of the Depression. The war
also gave blacks more opportunity to
fight for their rights.

World War II

The war started in Europe when the German Nazis under Adolf Hitler began to invade neighboring countries. By 1938 the United States was preparing to enter the war on the side of its European allies. Factories that made war materials were humming all across the country, but blacks had few opportunities to get jobs in these industries.

In January 1941, black leaders led by A. Philip Randolph went to Washington to meet with President Roosevelt. They

Tuskegee airmen receive their wings during promotion exercises.

Lt. Col. Benjamin Davis (right) talks with Lt. Charles W. Dryden (cockpit) before his solo mission in a P-40 fighter plane.

told him that unless he called for an end to discrimination in the defense industries, they would bring 100,000 blacks to the capital and stage a huge protest on the White House lawn. In June, the president signed Executive Order No. 8802, which stated, "There shall be no discrimination in the employment of workers in defense industries and in Government, because of race, creed, color, or national origin."

While this executive order did not end discrimination, it helped blacks gain more rights to equal employment.

Black leaders also pushed for an end to segregation in the armed forces after Japan attacked the U.S. naval base at

Pearl Harbor, Hawaii, in December 1941, and the United States officially entered the war. Many blacks had enlisted in the armed forces to help fight for the American cause, but they had always been assigned noncombat duties.

During the war, black soldiers fought for the first time in combat units in the Navy, Marines, and Army Air Corps. A special flying school was set up at Tuskegee Institute. The 99th Fighter Squadron, made up of pilots trained at Tuskegee, performed so well in European combat that they helped bring about the eventual integration of the Air Corps.

A. Philip Randolph, Bayard Rustin,

Two servicemen travel by tank to deliver mail to United States armed forces during the Korean War.

President Harry Truman receives an official report from his Civil Rights Commission in 1947, urging that racial segregation be wiped out of American life.

and other black leaders began a campaign to integrate the armed forces. President Roosevelt had died, and Vice President Harry S Truman became president in 1945. The leaders visited President Truman and threatened a massive protest unless the military was integrated. In 1948, President Truman ordered that the armed forces be integrated. The next time the United States went to war, in Korea in 1950, blacks and whites fought together. President Truman took other steps to guarantee greater rights for African Americans. He appointed a Civil Rights Commission to study the problems of discrimination and segregation.

There was still segregation in other parts of the country besides the South, and during the war years another group was formed to fight for black rights. The Congress of Racial Equality (CORE)

was formed in 1942 by James Farmer, Bayard Rustin, and a group of students at the University of Chicago. CORE pioneered the use of the sit-in as a tactic of protest by staging such a demonstration at a restaurant in Chicago.

During the war years, some whites began to change their minds about whether or not blacks deserved to enjoy equal citizenship rights. They believed, as blacks did, that if blacks fought bravely for their country, they should enjoy equal rights at home. But others, especially in the South, feared that returning veterans would feel as if they were entitled to equal rights. As a result, racial discrimination increased.

The industries that had been busy supporting the war effort had to lay off workers, and black workers were the first to be let go.

Bayard Rustin, a leading civil rights activist who served as Dr. King's assistant and helped organize the first Freedom Rides and the March on Washington.

James Farmer, founder of the Congress of Racial Equality (CORE), and former assistant secretary of Health, Education, and Welfare.

"With All Deliberate Speed"

By 1950 the NAACP had been working for decades to win more rights for blacks through the courts. It had been a long, uphill fight, and there had been very few real successes. The NAACP had concentrated on the area of education and had been disappointed time and again in its fight to force southern state colleges and universities to admit black students. Each time the NAACP proved discrimination, the southern states would simply establish a separate, and inferior, college for blacks.

Finally, the NAACP decided to attack the whole issue of "separate but equal" education and prove that separate schools were not equal. Charles Hamilton Houston, dean of the Law School at the all-black Howard University in Washington, D.C., trained hundreds of black

Linda Brown stands in front of the Sumner school in Topeka, Kansas, marking the tenth anniversary of the historic Supreme Court decision in the Brown vs Topeka Board of Education case.

lawyers to join this fight. The most famous was Thurgood Marshall, who later became the first African American Supreme Court justice.

Marshall went to work for the NAACP and founded a separate legal branch of the organization. In 1954, he and other NAACP attorneys argued the case of *Brown v. Topeka (Kansas) Board of Education* before the United States Supreme Court. They proved that the school boards spent more money on the white schools than on the black, that black schools were always more run-down and had fewer books and supplies than white schools. Some of the most powerful testimony in the case came from experts who showed that black children were psychologically hurt by segregation.

Lawyers George E.C. Hayes, Thurgood Marshall, and James M. Nabrit (left to right), after the court's announcement of its decision declaring segregation unconstitutional.

A long line of African Americans gather outside the United States Supreme Court during the Brown vs Topeka Board of Education hearings.

"All the News That's Fit to Print"

The New York Times.

LATE CITY EDITION
Fair and cool today. Mostly sunny, continued cool tomorrow.
Temperature Range Today-Max., 68; Min., 52
Temperatures Yesterday—Max., 69; Min., 61
Full U. S. Weather Bureau Report, Page 51

VOL. CIII ... No. 35,178. Entered as Second-Class Matter. Post Office, New York, N. Y. NEW YORK, TUESDAY, MAY 18, 1954. Times Square, New York 36, N. Y. Telephone LAckawanna 4-1000 FIVE CENTS

HIGH COURT BANS SCHOOL SEGREGATION; 9-TO-0 DECISION GRANTS TIME TO COMPLY

McCarthy Hearing Off a Week as Eisenhower Bars Report

SENATOR IS IRATE

President Orders Aides Not to Disclose Details of Top-Level Meeting

President's letter and excerpts from transcript, Pages 24, 25, 26.

By W. H. LAWRENCE
Special to The New York Times.

WASHINGTON, May 17—A secrecy directive by President Eisenhower resulted today in an abrupt recess for at least a week of the Senate's Army-McCarthy hearings.

Democratic and Republican Senators, some publicly and some privately, predicted that the investigation might never resume in earnest. However, there were other Senators who insisted that the investigation would go on to completion.

The recess was voted after Herbert Brownell Jr., the Attorney General, disclosed formally that criminal prosecutions might be instituted against those involved in the "preparation and dissemination" of an altered, condensed but still confidential Federal Bureau of Investigation report. This was offered in evidence last week by Senator Joseph R. McCarthy, Republican of Wisconsin.

Republicans outvoted Democrats 4 to 3 on the Senate Permanent Subcommittee of Investigation to recess the hearings until 10 o'clock next Monday morning. They acted amid charges and denials that the way was being prepared for a "whitewash."

Constitutional Division Cited

President Eisenhower cited the constitutional separation of powers between the Executive and Legislative branches in directing that details and conversations at a "high level" Administration meeting on Jan. 21 must be withheld from the committee.

Testimony already has been given that top White House, Justice and Defense officials had made plans at that conference to deal with Senator McCarthy.

The Presidential order served effectively to seal the lips of John G. Adams, the Army's regular counselor, about what Sherman Adams, the chief Presidential assistant, said to him in advising that a written report be prepared on how Senator McCarthy and his chief counsel, Roy M. Cohn, persistenly sought preferential treatment for Pvt. G. David Schine.

Before his induction, Mr. Schine was an unpaid consultant to the McCarthy subcommittee, the same group that is now conducting the hearings under the temporary chairmanship of Senator Karl E. Mundt, Republican of South Dakota.

Senator McCarthy angrily denounced today's Eisenhower order as "an Iron Curtain." His ire was shared, but in more restrained terms, by all the Republican and Democratic members of the investigating committee.

The week's postponement of

Continued on Page 24, Column 1

Communist Arms Unloaded in Guatemala By Vessel From Polish Port, U. S. Learns

State Department Views News Gravely Because of Red Infiltration

Special to The New York Times.

WASHINGTON, May 17—The State Department said today that it had reliable information that "an important shipment of arms' had been sent from Communist-controlled territory to Guatemala.

It said the arms, now being unloaded at Puerto Barrios, Guatemala, had been shipped from Stettin, a former German Baltic seaport, which has been occupied by Communist Poland since World War II. The Guatemalan regime has been frequently accused of being influenced by Communists.

"Because of the origin of these arms, the point of their embarkation, their destination and the

The New York Times May 18, 1954
Site of arms arrival (cross)

quantity of arms involved, the Department of State considers that this is a development of gravity," the announcement said.

A freighter arrived at Puerto

Embassy Says Nation of Central America May Buy Munitions Anywhere

Barrios last Saturday, the State Department reported, carrying a large shipment of armament consigned to the Guatemalan Government.

The State Department did not divulge the exact quantity of the arms, their nature or where they had been manufactured.

Reliable sources told The New York Times, however, that ten freight car loads of goods listed in the manifest as "hardware" had been unloaded from this ship and sent to the city of Guatemala since Sunday. Guatemala is 150 miles from Puerto Barrios. The

Continued on Page 10, Column 5

SOVIET BIDS VIENNA CEASE 'INTRIGUES'

Envoy Warns Austrian Chief on Inciting East Zone—Raab Denies Charges

By JOHN MacCORMAC
Special to The New York Times.

VIENNA, May 17—The Soviet Union warned Austria today to put an end to "hostile and subversive intrigues" against the Soviet occupation forces, or Soviet authorities would do it themselves.

Ivan I. Ilyichev, Soviet High Commissioner, reverted to a practice of early post-war days by summoning Chancellor Julius Raab and Vice Chancellor Adolf Schaerf to give them this warning. The Chancellor denied the Soviet charges.

Mr. Ilyichev said the Austrian Government had been guilty of staging actions hostile to the Soviet while the Austrian press had published daily slanderous and inciting announcements about the Soviet Union and Soviet occupation troops.

The cessation of Soviet control over the movement of freight, said the High Commissioner, was abused to smuggle militarist literature and provocative incitements into the Soviet zone with the connivance of the Austrian Minister of Interior.

When Soviet authorities ordered the removal of anti-Soviet placards in their zone, the minister instructed his subordinates to disregard the order and the Government approved his action, said Mr. Ilyichev.

He added that the Government, and particularly the Minister of Interior, had tolerated militarist propaganda by former soldiers' organizations and dissemination of propaganda for another Anschluss (union) with Germany.

The High Commissioner reminded the Government leaders that since Austria had not ob-

Continued on Page 9, Column 3

City Colleges' Board Can't Pick Chairman

The Board of Higher Education was unable to elect a chairman at its annual meeting last night at Hunter College.

A spokesman said it was the first time "within memory of board officials" that such a situation had occurred.

Nineteen of the twenty-one members of the board, which governs the four municipal colleges, attended.

Two members nominated for the one-year-term were unable to attain the required majority of eleven votes. They were Joseph B. Cavallaro, who was up for re-election as chairman, and Dr. Harry J. Carman, who was restored to the board on March 2 by Mayor Wagner.

The election was laid over until June 15.

INDO-CHINA PARLEY WEIGHS TWO PLANS

French and Rebel Peace Bids Will Be Studied Jointly as a Basis for Settlement

By THOMAS J. HAMILTON
Special to The New York Times.

GENEVA, May 17—The Far East conference decided today to take up French and Vietminh proposals jointly as a basis for settlement of the war in Indo-China.

The secret session, which lasted three and a half hours, was generally recognized as the opening round in what may turn out to be a long process of negotiation. Another secret meeting will be held tomorrow.

Western delegates felt that Vyacheslav M. Molotov, Soviet Foreign Minister, was continuing to give the impression that in the end he might throw Moscow's influence on the side of an agreed settlement.

However, the West failed to obtain answers to the two fundamental questions that are expected to determine whether the negotiations here will have any chance of success: Will the Communists agree to a separate settlement for Laos and Cambodia, and will they agree to an armistice in Vietnam without at the same time requiring a political settlement?

The conference will address itself tomorrow to the issue of Laos and Cambodia. The two Indo-Chinese states are relatively free from Communist infiltration, and their leaders contend, with the support of the French, that the only thing that needs to be done is the withdrawal of the Communists.

The Laos-Cambodia and Vietnam issues were discussed inconclusively today after the delegates had devoted the first part of their meeting to the intricate dispute over evacuation of French Union wounded from Dienbienphu, seized by the Communist-

Continued on Page 2, Column 2

2 TAX PROJECTS DIE IN ESTIMATE BOARD

Beer Levy and More Parking Collections Killed—Payroll Impost Still Weighed

By CHARLES G. BENNETT

Two possible new revenue sources were definitely eliminated yesterday by the Board of Estimate in executive session. They were the proposed 1-cent-a-glass tax on beer and the suggestion to extend metered parking into hours now "free."

In a three-hour City Hall parley the board failed once more to decide on a new impost or imposts to balance the 1954-55 budget of $1,639,438,325. Mayor Wagner said after the meeting that the highly controversial 3 per cent sales tax on commercial services was "still one of the taxes at the top of the list."

Saying he felt the Board of Estimate was close to a decision on the knotty tax question, the Mayor added that "there's no decision to discard any tax" except the two mentioned above, and that at the same time "no tax is inevitable."

The board will wrestle with the tax question again in executive session on Thursday at 2:30 P. M. The Mayor said the City Council, which is holding up a bill to impose the sales tax extension, would be invited to send a delegation to the Thursday session.

Mr. Wagner asserted that he would like to see the Board of Estimate decide the tax question

Continued on Page 32, Column 5

REACTION OF SOUTH

'Breathing Spell' for Adjustment Tempers Region's Feelings

By JOHN N. POPHAM
Special to The New York Times.

CHATTANOOGA, Tenn., May 17—The South's reaction to the Supreme Court's decision outlawing racial segregation in public schools appeared to be tempered considerably today.

The time lag allowed for carrying out the required transitions seemed to be the major factor in that reaction.

Southern leaders of both races in political, educational and community service fields expressed comment that covered a wide range. Some spoke bitter words that verged on defiance. Others ranged from sharp disagreement to predictions of peaceful and successful adjustment in accord with the ruling.

But underneath the surface of much of the comment, it was evident that many Southerners recognized that the decision had laid down the legal principle rejecting segregation in public education facilities.

They also noted that it had left open a challenge to the region to join in working out a program of necessary changes in the present bi-racial school systems.

Three of the most illustrative viewpoints were those expressed by Govs. James F. Byrnes of South Carolina and Herman Talmadge of Georgia, and Harold Fleming, a spokesman for the Southern Regional Council, the most effective interracial organization in the South.

Byrnes Sees Reversal

Governor Byrnes, who has vigorously defended the doctrine of separate but equal facilities in education, said that he was "shocked to learn that the court has reversed itself" with regard to past rulings on that doctrine.

However, Governor Byrnes, a former Associate Justice of the Supreme Court, noted that the tribunal had not yet delivered its final decree setting forth the time and terms for ending segregation in the schools.

Pointing out that South Carolina, a party in the litigation before the court, had until October to present arguments on how the Supreme Court should order the implementation of the decision, Governor Byrnes declared "I urge all of our people, white and colored, to exercise restraint and preserve order."

Governor Talmadge repeatedly has vowed there "will never be mixed schools while I am Governor" and has warned that school integration would lead to "blood-

Continued on Page 20, Column 1

Associated Press Wirephoto

LEADERS IN SEGREGATION FIGHT: Lawyers who led battle before U. S. Supreme Court for abolition of segregation in public schools congratulate one another as they leave court after announcement of decision. Left to right: George E. C. Hayes, Thurgood Marshall and James M. Nabrit.

MORETTIS' LAWYER MUST BARE TALKS

Jersey Court Orders Counsel to Racketeers in Bergen to Divulge Data to Grand Jury

By GEORGE CABLE WRIGHT
Special to The New York Times.

TRENTON, May 17—The New Jersey Supreme Court today ordered a lawyer who once had represented top Bergen County racketeers to divulge to a grand jury the substance of confidential talks with those clients.

The four-to-three decision reversed the rulings of two lower courts. Involved was the refusal more than a year ago of John E. Selser, Hackensack attorney, to answer four questions put to him by the Bergen County grand jury.

Mr. Selser told the jury that one of his clients, Willie Moretti, slain gambler, had given him the names of persons connected with Walter G. Winne who had received protection money from syndicate gamblers. Mr. Winne, superseded prosecutor of Bergen County, was acquitted last week of nonfeasance in office.

But the attorney balked when asked to reveal these and the names of other persons who, his clients alleged, had been paid protection money or who had received political contributions on the state and county level. He pleaded that his lips were sealed by the duty of "nondisclosure of confidential communications between client and attorney."

Represented Morettis, Others

Mr. Selser had represented Moretti, who was murdered in Cliffside Park in October, 1951, and his brother, the late Salvatore Moretti, for many years. He also was the attorney of record for Joe Adonis, Arthur Longano and James (Piggy) Lynch. The last four were among five men convicted and sent to prison in May, 1952, as the leaders of the Bergen gambling syndicate.

Mr. Selser appeared before the grand jury in February, 1953. The present court action was brought by the state after his refusal to answer the above questions on that occasion and two other questions. The latter pertained to testimony by John J. Dickerson, former Republican state chairman, before the same grand jury.

Mr. Dickerson had testified that Adonis and the two Morettis visited his home in November, 1950, and that Willie told him then that $225,000 in protection money had been paid to Harold

Continued on Page 36, Column 2

RULING TO FIGURE IN '54 CAMPAIGN

Decision Tied to Eisenhower—Russell Leads Southerners in Criticism of Court

By WILLIAM S. WHITE
Special to The New York Times

WASHINGTON, May 17—Congress as a whole grappled gingerly today with the profound political implications of the Supreme Court's anti-segregation decision.

It became clear at once—and by both parties was accepted in private as inevitable—that the court's action would figure importantly in the coming Congressional election campaigns.

Publicly, however, the Republicans and the non-Southern Democrats, on the whole maintained silence. The Southerners, all angry or sorrowing in one degree or another, were quickly articulate and split among themselves into at least three factions.

¶One Southern group, by all the indications not a large one, was openly defiant of the court, as typified by the comment of Senator James O. Eastland of Mississippi.

"The South," Mr. Eastland said, "will not abide by nor obey this legislative decision by a political court."

¶A second Southern group, while not openly challenging the court, began to threaten efforts to force an alteration of its view, as illustrated by the comment of

Continued on Page 20, Column 2

1896 RULING UPSET

'Separate but Equal' Doctrine Held Out of Place in Education

Text of Supreme Court decision is printed on Page 15.

By LUTHER A. HUSTON
Special to The New York Times.

WASHINGTON, May 17—The Supreme Court unanimously outlawed today racial segregation in public schools.

Chief Justice Earl Warren read two opinions that put the stamp of unconstitutionality on school systems in twenty-one states and the District of Columbia where segregation is permissive or mandatory.

The court, taking cognizance of the problems involved in the integration of the school systems concerned, put over until the next term, beginning in October, the formulation of decrees to effectuate its 9-to-0 decision.

The opinions set aside the "separate but equal" doctrine laid down by the Supreme Court in 1896.

"In the field of public education," Chief Justice Warren said, "the doctrine of 'separate but equal' has no place. Separate educational facilities are inherently unequal."

He stated the question and supplied the answer as follows:

"We come then to the question presented: Does segregation of children in public schools solely on the basis of race, even though physical facilities and other 'tangible' factors may be equal, deprive the children of the minority group of equal educational opportunities? We believe that it does."

States Stressed Rights

The court's opinion does not apply to private schools. It is directed entirely at public schools. It does not affect the "separate but equal doctrine" as applied on railroads and other public carriers entirely within states that have such restrictions.

The principal ruling of the court was in four cases involving state laws. The states' right to operate separated schools had been argued before the court on two occasions by representatives of South Carolina, Virginia, Kansas and Delaware.

In these cases, consolidated in one opinion, the high court held that school segregation deprived Negroes of "the equal protection of the laws guaranteed by the Fourteenth Amendment."

The other opinion involved the District of Columbia. Here schools have been segregated since Civil War days under laws passed by Congress.

"In view of our decision that the Constitution prohibits the states from maintaining racially segregated public schools," the Chief Justice said, "it would be unthinkable that the same Constitution would impose a lesser duty on the Federal Government.

"We hold that racial segregation in the public schools of the District of Columbia is a denial

Continued on Page 14, Column 6

Churchill Asks Negotiated Peace With Guarantees for Indo-China

By DREW MIDDLETON
Special to The New York Times.

LONDON, May 17—Britain will seek effective international guarantees for any peace settlement in Indo-China, Prime Minister Churchill declared today.

Negotiation of an "acceptable" settlement at the Geneva conference remains the immediate task of the British Government, Sir Winston emphasized in a statement to the House of Commons.

Until the outcome of that conference is known, he added, "final decisions" cannot be taken by the Government about the establishment of a collective defense system in Southeast Asia and the Western Pacific.

Peace by negotiation emerged from Sir Winston's cautious statement as the only policy that the Cabinet was ready to apply to the problem of Indo-China. Observers were struck by the fact that, aside from the Prime Minister's reference to the necessity of backing a settlement there with guarantees, the British position was substantially the same as when the Geneva conference began.

[Indonesia is considering asking India and Burma to join her in a nonaggression treaty with Communist China as a means of offsetting United States plans for a Southeast Asian alliance.]

Sir Winston's adherence to negotiation is acceptable to both major parties in the Commons,

Continued on Page 4, Column 3

Costello Is Sentenced to 5 Years, Fined $30,000 in U. S. Tax Case

By EDWARD RANZAL

Frank Costello was sentenced yesterday by Federal Judge John F. X. McGohey to five years in jail and fined $30,000 for income tax evasion.

The dapper, 61-year-old gambler was remanded immediately. Later Judge Harold R. Medina in the United States Court of Appeals refused to set bail pending appeal. Costello, who listened to the sentencing in icy-calm manner, was taken to the Federal House of Detention, 427 West Street.

Besides the jail sentence and the fines, Judge McGohey also assessed Costello for court costs. Lloyd F. MacMahon, chief assistant United States Attorney, said the costs would be about $5,000, only a fraction of what it cost the Government in its investigation, which began in earnest in 1952.

Costello was convicted Thursday night by a Federal court jury of five women and seven men of three counts of a four-count indictment. They found the gambler guilty of evading a total of $51,095 in taxes from 1947 through 1949.

In 1947 Costello evaded $22,563; in 1948, $13,786, and in 1949, $14,746. He was acquitted of the charge of evading taxes in 1946. Costello's attorney, Leo C. Fennelly, told Judge McGohey that the acquittal on this count meant that the gambler was entitled to a refund for that year.

Before the sentencing Mr. MacMahon said that for years Costello had schemed to cheat the Government out of taxes. He added that the gambler had concealed at least $140,000 of his income from 1947 through 1949, more than half his income.

Mr. MacMahon contended that Costello, by devious means, had concealed the receipt of his income as well as the source by using cash in every transaction where it was possible.

Evidence at the six-week trial, the prosecutor said, showed that from 1937 through 1945 Costello deliberately underestimated his income by at least $202,000. The statute of limitations, he added, bars prosecution for the earlier tax evasions.

"Costello has spent a lifetime making money on the shady side

Continued on Page 36, Column 4

'Voice' Speaks in 34 Languages To Flash Court Ruling to World

Within an hour after the Supreme Court decision on school segregation yesterday afternoon, the Voice of America sent a news broadcast by shortwave to Eastern Europe.

The decision came in time for the regularly scheduled "World-wide English Broadcast" at 2 o'clock. The broadcast was written in English on the Voice's central desk and was sent by teletype to the thirty-four language desks.

There it was translated and sent out in various foreign tongues all over the world as broadcast time arrived for each.

"The Supreme Court has ruled unanimously," the Voice said in its broadcast, "that racial segregation has no place in American public education. It held that separation of students on a racial basis denies equal educational opportunities.

"Chief Justice [Earl] Warren, reading the court's findings, said that the doctrine of providing separate but equal facilities has no place in public education. Separation of children solely because of race, he said, generates feelings in their hearts and minds which might never be undone. * * *

"The ruling in effect outlaws all segregation in public schools throughout the United States. The court held that to separate students is a denial of the due process of law guaranteed by the Fifth Amendment to the Constitution and equal opportunity

Continued on Page 15, Column 4

A National Guardsman points Elizabeth Echford toward Central High School on her first day at the all white school.

The Supreme Court justices ruled that segregated education was unconstitutional and ordered that segregated school districts integrate "with all deliberate speed." But there was great resistance to the idea of integrated schools in the South. Several state governors defied court orders to integrate, insisting that the federal government could not force the states to integrate. In 1957, President Dwight D. Eisenhower had to order federal troops to Little Rock, Arkansas, to escort nine black students to the previously all-white Central High School.

It would take many years before the Supreme Court's ruling was obeyed, and today there are still many schools that are not integrated. Still, the *Brown v. Board of Education* case was a major blow against segregation.

Six of the nine students who integrated Central High School in Little Rock, Arkansas. Top (l to r): Gloria Ray, Terrance Roberts, and Melba Pattillo. Bottom (l to r): Jefferson Thomas, Carlotta Walls, and Thelma Mothershed.

The New York Times.

VOL. CVII..No. 36,404.   © 1957 by The New York Times Company. Times Square, New York 36, N. Y.   NEW YORK, WEDNESDAY, SEPTEMBER 25, 1957.   the beyond 100-mile zone from New York City   FIVE CENTS

PRESIDENT SENDS TROOPS TO LITTLE ROCK, FEDERALIZES ARKANSAS NATIONAL GUARD; TELLS NATION HE ACTED TO AVOID ANARCHY

WEST AGAIN BARS SOVIET PROPOSAL ON MIDEAST TALK

U. S. Says Latest Moscow Note 'Cynically Distorts' American Action

Text of U. S. note to Soviet will be found on Page 5.

By DANA ADAMS SCHMIDT
Special to The New York Times

WASHINGTON, Sept. 24.—The United States, Britain and France rejected today the latest in a series of Soviet bids for recognition of the Soviet Union's role in the Middle East.

A brief United States reply delivered in Moscow today said a Soviet note of Sept. 3 was "offensive in tone and cynically distorts United States objectives and actions in the Middle East."

It accused the Soviet Union of setting in motion "a chain of events leading to the present dangerous situation" by shipping large quantities of arms into the area.

U. S. Affirms Doctrine

The note warned the Soviet Union that the United States Government intended to carry out the national policy laid down in the Eisenhower Doctrine, which "regards the preservation of the independence and integrity of the nations of that region as vital to world peace and as vital, therefore, to its own national interests."

The doctrine, proclaimed in a Joint Resolution of the House of Representatives and the Senate on March 9, 1957, also affirmed the President's authority to use United States forces to aid any Middle East state that asked for help against aggression by a power controlled by international communism.

The Soviet Union's note has accused the United States of seeking to overthrow the Syrian Government and of generally fomenting trouble in the Middle East.

3d Rejection of Soviet Bid

It had proposed, for the third time, a four-power declaration renouncing the use of force in the area. Earlier Soviet proposals for such a declaration, all rejected by the West, were made Feb. 11 and April 19.

As interpreted by United States experts on the Middle East, these notes were meant to convey the idea that the four powers should meet to negotiate a settlement of their rivalries in the Middle East. The first of the notes even went into detail with a proposal for an embargo on shipment of arms to the area.

Because the Soviet Union has asserted its presence in Syria, and because there seems to be little the Western powers can do to reverse developments in the area,

Continued on Page 5, Column 3

SOVIET ASSAILED BY LLOYD AT U. N.

Briton Suggests Arms Sent Arabs May Be Stocks for Future Bases

Excerpts from Lloyd's speech are printed on Page 4.

By THOMAS J. HAMILTON
Special to The New York Times

UNITED NATIONS, N. Y., Sept. 24.—Britain announced today that Soviet arms shipments to Arab countries. Selwyn Lloyd, British Foreign Secretary, suggested that the purpose might be to "pre-stock forward bases for the Soviet Union itself."

Mr. Lloyd told the General Assembly that Soviet arms had been delivered "on such a scale as to give some color to this suggestion." He added that Britain viewed the Syrian situation "with grave concern." In addition, he criticized Soviet policy throughout the area.

Mr. Lloyd devoted most of his speech to the Middle East and to disarmament. He did not say what action the Assembly should take on either subject.

However, he declared that Britain would be 25 cents a

Continued on Page 4, Column 4

London and Bonn Rule Out Any Currency Revaluation

Britain Tells Monetary Fund Session She Will Draw $500,000,000 in Stand-By Credit From Export-Import Bank

By EDWIN L. DALE JR.
Special to The New York Times

WASHINGTON, Sept. 24.—British and West German spokesmen and the Managing Director of the International Monetary Fund said today that the question of exchange rates for the pound and the mark was "definitely settled." There will be no change.

Both the British and the West Germans emphasized that the recent huge flow of gold and dollars out of Britain and into West Germany had been based solely on speculation, not on basic factors in their foreign trading accounts.

Per Jacobsson, the Fund's Managing Director, said: "The growing knowledge that there will be no alteration in the value of either the Deutsche

neycroft indicated that Britain was drawing the money to demonstrate to speculators that she had the resources to defend the pound.

At the same time, Britain, through Peter Thorneycroft, Chancellor of the Exchequer, announced she would draw $500,000,000 stand-by credit she arranged last winter with the United States Export-Import Bank.

In his speech at the annual meeting of the fund, Mr. Thor-

Continued on Page 8, Column 2

City Approves Plan By Wiley to Build Midtown Garages

By JOSEPH C. INGRAHAM

The Board of Estimate has approved in principle the program of Traffic Commissioner T. T. Wiley for garage construction in the heart of lower and mid-Manhattan.

The decision clears the way for a start on $24,000,000 of garages it also sets a three-year dispute between Mr. Wiley and other city executives that has stymied off-street parking relief.

As a result, the first of the projects—a garage in the Herald Square area—will be the space for 610 cars on eight levels. Eight other garages are to be centrally located in Manhattan and two in the busiest parts of the Bronx.

The Herald Square garage will be east of the Avenue of the Americas between West Thirty-fifth and Thirty-sixth Streets with entrances and exits on both streets. There will be space for 610 cars on eight levels accessible by ramps. Rates will be geared to "meet the heavy unsatisfied demand for short-time parking," Mr. Wiley said.

Rates proposed by the Commissioner would be 25 cents a

Continued on Page 33, Column 1

SOLDIERS FLY IN

1,000 Go to Little Rock —9,936 in Guard Told to Report

The texts of Executive orders on troops are on Page 16.

By JACK RAYMOND
Special to The New York Times

WASHINGTON, Sept. 24.—The Army ordered all Arkansas National Guardsmen to report for Federal duty tonight and rushed 1,000 airborne troops of the Regular Army into Little Rock to preserve order.

The Regulars were members of the 101st Airborne Division, which won fame in World War II under the command of Gen. Maxwell D. Taylor, now Chief of Staff of the Army.

Maj. Gen. Edwin A. Walker, a much-decorated combat commander with a reputation for toughness, was put in command of the Regular Army contingent and the federalized Guardsmen in Arkansas. He is the commander of the Arkansas Military District.

General Walker's mission is to make sure that no one frustrates Federal order that nine Negro pupils be admitted to Central High School.

Wilson Carries Out Order

Charles E. Wilson, Secretary of Defense, carrying out President Eisenhower's mandate, earlier had called the entire Arkansas Army and Air National Guard, totaling 9,936 men, into Federal service.

The Secretary of Defense and Wilber M. Brucker, Secretary of the Army, acted two hours after President Eisenhower's executive order authorizing "all appropriate steps" to make school attendance possible for the Negroes who had been admitted to the high school.

However, an Army spokesman said that it was planned to make "the absolute minimum demonstration of force necessary."

Immediately after Secretary Wilson signed the federalization call to the Arkansas Guard at 2:25 P. M., Secretary Brucker telephoned the office of Gov. Orval E. Faubus in Little Rock.

At the same time he sent a telegram to the Governor, explaining that President Eisenhower "desires" the personnel of the Arkansas Army and Air National Guard organizations

Continued on Page 14, Column 2

SOLDIERS IN LITTLE ROCK: Residents of Arkansas capital looking on last night as men of the 101st Airborne Division took positions outside the Central High School.

GOVERNORS URGE WHITE HOUSE TALK

Southerners Move to Set Up Mediation Machinery in Use of Federal Troops

By JOHN N. POPHAM
Special to The New York Times

SEA ISLAND, Ga., Sept. 24.—Southern Governors moved tonight to establish mediation machinery that would remove Federal troops from the South. The Governors acted a few hours after President Eisenhower federalized the Arkansas National Guard.

Gov. Luther Hodges of North Carolina, chairman of the Southern Governors Conference in session here, announced that two proposals would be submitted to the resolutions committee of the conference for formal consideration tomorrow.

One is a proposal of Gov. Frank G. Clement of Tennessee to establish an informal committee of Southern Governors to seek a meeting with President Eisenhower in a search for a solution to the Little Rock school integration crisis.

The other is a request to the President to hold off the use of Federal troops and to give

Continued on Page 16, Column 2

Troops on Guard at School; Negroes Ready to Return

By BENJAMIN FINE
Special to The New York Times

LITTLE ROCK, Ark., Sept. 24.—Troops from the Army's crack 101st Airborne Division, carrying carbines and billy clubs, took posts around Central High School tonight. They were here to see that court-ordered integration is carried out.

With police sirens wailing and headlights flashing, Army trucks loaded with soldiers roared into position. The soldiers represented about a quarter of the contingent of 1,000 crack troops of the division that was ordered to Little Rock by President Eisenhower to prevent mob riots and violence.

The first group of 500 airborne soldiers came to the city this afternoon from Fort Campbell, Ky., and a second group of 500 arrived by plane this evening. The bulk of the two groups bivouacked for the night in areas away from the school.

General Issues Order

Maj. Gen. Edwin A. Walker, commander of the Arkansas Military District, issued a formal order to the people of Little Rock not to collect in crowds and to let Central High School be integrated peaceably.

With the arrival of Federal troops, including some Negro soldiers who were not expected to be on duty at the school, Negro students were ready to try again to enter the high school.

A mask of 1,000 persons yesterday forced the city and school authorities to have the nine Negro students who had attended integrated classes for 3 hours and 13 minutes. The students did not try to enter the school today.

Mrs. L. C. Bates, president

Continued on Page 15, Column 1

Price Index Up .2%; Sets Another High

By RICHARD E. MOONEY
Special to The New York Times

WASHINGTON, Sept. 24.—The United States Consumers' Price Index rose two-tenths of a per cent in August, setting another record. It was the twelfth consecutive monthly increase, but among the smallest of the twelve.

The Labor Department's Bureau of Labor Statistics reported today that the index rose in August to 121, using the average in the 1947-49 period as a comparison base of 100. All the major categories of prices increased, but food and housing were the strongest factors.

The August index was 3.6 per cent higher than that of a year earlier. This meant that a typical city family paid $1.03.3.5 in August of 1957 for the goods and services that cost $1 in August of 1956.

The Commerce Department

Continued on Page 24, Column 3

EISENHOWER ON AIR

Says School Defiance Has Gravely Harmed Prestige of U. S.

Text of President's address appears on Page 14.

By ANTHONY LEWIS
Special to The New York Times

WASHINGTON, Sept. 24.—President Eisenhower sent Federal troops to Little Rock, Ark., today to open the way for the admission of nine Negro pupils to Central High School.

Earlier, the President federalized the Arkansas National Guard and authorized calling the Guard and regular Federal forces to remove obstructions to justice in Little Rock school integration.

His history-making action was based on a formal finding that his "cease and desist" proclamation, issued last night, had not been obeyed. Mobs of pro-segregationists still gathered in the vicinity of Central High School this morning.

Tonight, from the White House, President Eisenhower told the nation in a speech for radio and television that he had acted to prevent "mob rule" and "anarchy."

Historic Decision

The President's decision to send troops to Little Rock was reached as his vacation base reached at his vacation headquarters in Newport, R. I. It was one of historic importance politically, socially, constitutionally. For the first time since the Reconstruction days that followed the Civil War, the Federal Government was using its ultimate power to compel equal treatment of the Negro in the South.

He said violent defiance of Federal Court orders on Little Rock had done grave harm to "the prestige and influence, and indeed to the safety, of our nation and the world." He called on the people of Arkansas and, indeed the whole country, "to preserve and respect the law even when they disagree with it."

Guardsmen Withdrawn

Action quickly followed the President's orders. During the day and night 1,000 members of the 101st Airborne Division were flown to Little Rock. Charles E. Wilson, Secretary of Defense, ordered into Federal service all 10,000 members of the Arkansas National Guard.

Today's events were the climax of three weeks of skirmishing between the Federal Government and Gov. Orval E Faubus of Arkansas. It was three weeks ago this morning that the Governor first ordered National Guard troops to Central High School to preserve order. The nine Negro students were prevented from entering the school.

The Guardsmen were gone yesterday, withdrawn by Governor Faubus as the result of a

Continued on Page 14, Column 6

CONGRESS IS SPLIT ON USE OF TROOPS

Johnston Calls for Faubus to Resist President but Others Hail His Move

By JOHN W. FINNEY
Special to The New York Times

WASHINGTON, Sept. 24.—Congressional reaction to President Eisenhower's decision to use troops in the Little Rock integration crisis ranged from angry denunciation to outright praise today.

Southern Senators sharply criticized the President and suggested he had exceeded his legal authority. Northern Senators supported the President, but some of them expressed reservations that the action was rather belated.

Expects Faubus to Act

Senator Olin D. Johnston, Democrat of South Carolina, suggested that Gov. Orval E Faubus of Arkansas "stand up for states' rights" and force a showdown with the President by calling on the Arkansas National Guard on duty.

Senator Johnston, a former Governor of South Carolina, said if he were Governor Faubus, "I'd proclaim a state of insurrection down there, and I'd call out the National Guard. And I'd then find out what's going to run things in my state."

Asked by reporters whether he believed Governor Faubus would take such steps, Senator Johnston said, "I think he will and I hope he will."

Aiken Defends Move

Senator John L. McClellan, Democrat of Arkansas, said he believed such use of military force by the Federal Government was "without authority of law."

He said he was "very apprehensive that such action may precipitate more trouble than it will prevent."

Senator Richard B. Russell, Democrat of Georgia and leader of Southern opposition to the Civil Rights Bill in the last session, said that President Eisenhower's use of troops might "put Negro children in the schools," but that it would "have a calamitous effect on race relations and on the cause of national unity."

On the other side of the issue Senator George D. Aiken, Republican of Vermont, said the President "is undoubtedly within

Continued on Page 17, Column 3

Textile Union Gets 30 Days to Reform

By A. H. RASKIN

A scandal-tainted textile union was ordered yesterday to oust its two chief officers within thirty days or face possible suspension from the merged labor federation.

The ultimatum was given to the 40,000-member United Textile Workers by the executive council of the American Federation of Labor and Congress of Industrial Organizations.

It foreshadowed the fixing of a similar clean-up deadline today for the 1,400,000-member International Brotherhood of Teamsters and the 140,000-member Bakery and Confectionery Workers International Union.

The federation's Ethical Practices Committee has found all three unions guilty of violating the anti-racketeering provisions of the A. F. L.-C. I. O. constitution. The findings were based

Continued on Page 19, Column 3

U. S. Cutters Conquer Northwest Passage

3 Coast Guard Craft First of the Nation to Make Transit

By JOHN H. FENTON
Special to The New York Times

BOSTON, Sept. 24.—Two Coast Guard cutters were saluted in Boston Harbor today at the end of a successful mission to find a practical Northwest Passage—a route around the top of the North American Continent.

A third cutter, the Spar, proceeded directly to her home port at Bristol, R. I, to be welcomed there as the first United States vessel to circumnavigate the continent.

The cutters Storis, from Juneau, Alaska, and the Bramble, from Miami, Fla., put in here for their welcoming. They will continue their homeward voyages later in the week.

The three cutters were the first United States vessels to make the passage.

The shrill sirens of waterspouting fireboats and the deeper-throated whistles of other craft sounded a "well done" as the twin bulky cutters made their way up the harbor.

Ranking Coast Guard officers and civil officials joined with members of families of the crews in a dockside welcome as the cutters tied up at

Continued on Page 10, Column 1

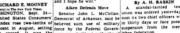

U. S. Coast Guard
Coast Guardsmen on the stern of the Spar view her sister cutters, Bramble, left, and Storis, during the transit of Simpson Strait. This was a difficult part of the voyage.

Rebel Chief Seized In Algiers Gunfight

By THOMAS F. BRADY
Special to The New York Times

ALGIERS, Algeria, Sept. 24.—The chief of the nationalist terrorist organization in Algiers was in the hands of French parachute troops today.

The rebel leader, Saadi Yacef, 29 years old, had eluded capture in the crowded Casbah for more than two years.

With him was 24-year-old Miss Zorah Drif, an Algerian revolutionary, who was condemned to death in absentia by a French military tribunal.

A parachute colonel told reporters this evening that Mr. Yacef and Miss Drif had surrendered at 5:30 A. M. after the terrorist shoot had wounded a lieutenant colonel and a master sergeant of a Foreign Legion parachute regiment. The colonel then took reporters to a hideout high in the Casbah where he described how the

Continued on Page 3, Column 2

Nonviolent Protest

Many black leaders felt that the way was now clear to attack other forms of segregation—on public transportation, in restaurants, and other public places. Mrs. Rosa Parks, a black woman in Montgomery, Alabama, was a member of the local NAACP, and she believed it was wrong for the city's bus company to make blacks sit in the back of the bus and force blacks to give up their seats to white riders. In December 1955, she refused to give up her seat on a bus to a white man and was arrested. Her arrest sparked the direct-action civil rights movement.

Tired of being pushed around, some of the black leaders in Montgomery formed an organization called the Montgomery Improvement Association (MIA) and called for a boycott of the buses to protest the arrest of Mrs. Parks and the segregation they were forced to endure. A young minister named Martin Luther King, Jr., was elected president of the MIA.

The MIA organized car pools and raised money so the local churches could buy vans to drive black workers to and from their jobs. Blacks who had no other form of transportation walked to where they needed to go. White employers fired blacks who refused to ride the buses. The lives of the boycott's leaders were threatened. Dr. King, who believed in the concept of nonviolence, counseled the protesters not to fight back. The blacks of Montgomery stayed off the buses for more than a year. Finally, the United States Supreme Court ruled that segregation on public buses was illegal.

Dr. King and other ministers believed

Rosa Parks is fingerprinted in jail after refusing to give up her seat to a white passenger in Montgomery, Alabama.

Dr. King joins members of the Montgomery bus boycott in a friendly conversation outside the E.L. Posey parking lot, one of the many depots serving Montgomery's black community during the boycott.

Reverend King addresses the Holt Street Baptist Church in a rousing speech where he vows the Montgomery bus boycott will continue, March 22, 1956.

they could bring about many more changes in the South through nonviolent protest. In 1957, with the assistance of A. Philip Randolph, they formed the Southern Christian Leadership Conference (SCLC) to campaign for civil rights in the South. In the spring of 1957 the SCLC, NAACP, and Randolph's Brotherhood of Sleeping Car Porters joined together in a prayer pilgrimage to Washington, D.C. There, on the steps of the Lincoln Memorial, King delivered his first major speech calling for voting rights for blacks.

That September, President Eisenhower signed into law the Civil Rights Act of 1957, the first civil rights legislation passed by Congress since Reconstruction. It created a Civil Rights Commission and established the Civil Rights Division of the Department of Justice. It also gave the federal government the power to enforce voting rights. But southern states resisted the idea of the federal government interfering in their affairs, and the government did little under the Civil Rights Act.

Still, as the decade of the 1950s drew to a close, African Americans were more hopeful than they had been since Reconstruction that real civil rights were within reach.

Sitting and Riding

The civil rights movement began to heat up on February 1, 1960, when students at the black North Carolina Agricultural and Technical College staged sit-ins at the local Woolworth's "whites only" lunch counter in an attempt to be served. Soon, black and white students in many parts of the country were engaging in sit-ins to desegregate other public places. A group of these students

College students from North Carolina A & T College stage a sit-in demonstration at the local F.W. Woolworth lunch counter in February of 1960.

got together and formed the Student Nonviolent Coordinating Committee. They agreed with Martin Luther King, Jr., that nonviolence was the best tactic for winning civil rights, but they did not feel he and the SCLC were activist enough.

In 1961, after the U.S. Supreme Court ruled that segregation in interstate bus terminal restaurants was unconstitutional, CORE began a series of Freedom Rides on interstate buses to the South to test whether the ruling was being obeyed. When the buses reached the

Freedom Riders John Lewis and Jim Zwerg after an attack in Montgomery, Alabama.

A Freedom Ride bus is set afire in Anniston, Alabama.

A dog attacks a young man during demonstrations in Birmingham, May 3, 1963.

Civil rights activists shield their bodies from the blast of high-powered fire hoses used by Birmingham's fire department.

Medgar Evers was shot and killed by a sniper in his driveway in 1963.

Eugene "Bull" Connor, Birmingham's police commissioner, who ordered the use of fire hoses and dogs on civil rights demonstrators in that city.

South, angry white mobs stoned the buses and beat the riders.

In 1962 several civil rights organizations combined to force desegregation of all public facilities in Albany, Georgia. That campaign failed.

The following year King and the SCLC organized a similar campaign in Birmingham, Alabama, which was successful. But the concept of nonviolence was sorely tested, as Birmingham police set dogs, and firemen turned their powerful water hoses on the protesters. June 12, 1963, also saw the brutal shooting of Medgar Evers, the NAACP Field Secretary for Mississippi.

Marching for Freedom

A. Philip Randolph and Bayard Rustin were concerned that the civil rights movement was moving away from the campaign for jobs and economic opportunity. They suggested a March on Washington for Jobs and Freedom. By the time the march occurred on August, 3, 1963, however, it had become a moral demonstration against evil. Organized by Bayard Rustin, the march brought an estimated 250,000 people, black and white, to the nation's capital. There, Dr. Martin Luther King, Jr., delivered his famous ''I Have a Dream'' speech, calling for peace between the races and equality for all people.

The march had a strong impact on the minds and hearts of many Americans. But so did the assassination of President John F. Kennedy in Novem-

While participating in voter registration drives in rural Mississippi during the summer of 1964, three civil rights workers, Michael Schwerner, James Chaney, and Andrew Goodman were kidnapped and murdered. Their bodies were discovered in graves near Philadelphia, Mississippi.

Dr. King waves to thousands of onlookers during the March on Washington in August of 1963.

A reenactment of the moment John F. Kennedy was shot in Dallas, Texas, November 22, 1963.

The outside of Birmingham's Sixteenth Street Baptist Church after the bombing of September 15, 1963. Four teenage girls were killed while attending Sunday school there.

ber of that year. Many people believed that the country was going to be destroyed by hate. On Sunday, September 15, 1963, when the Sixteenth Street Baptist Church of Birmingham, Alabama, was bombed, four young girls lost their lives. Hate was alive.

President Kennedy had planned to make civil rights a central part of his administration, and when Vice President Lyndon B. Johnson succeeded to the presidency, he vowed to carry out the slain president's wishes.

On July 2, 1964, President Johnson signed into law the most far-reaching civil rights legislation ever. The 1964 Civil Rights Act contained new provisions to help guarantee African Americans the right to vote and access to public accommodations. When southern states still tried to deny black people the vote, Johnson signed the 1965 Vot-

The New York Times.

VOL. CXIII...No. 38,864.

© 1964 by The New York Times Company.
Times Square, New York, N.Y. 10036

NEW YORK, SATURDAY, JUNE 20, 1964.

TEN CENTS

U.S. STRESSING IT WOULD FIGHT TO DEFEND ASIA

WARNING TO REDS

Commitment to Laos and South Vietnam Called Unlimited

By MAX FRANKEL
Special to The New York Times

WASHINGTON, June 19—The Administration is saying more emphatically each day that North Vietnam and its closest ally, Communist China, must leave their neighbors alone or face a war with the United States.

In the minds of officials here the United States commitment to the security of Southeast Asia is now unlimited and comparable with the commitment to West Berlin.

In diplomatic terms this means the officials most themselves unable to negotiate with anything except the threat of force to persuade the Asian Communists to stop the efforts to "liberate" South Vietnam and Laos.

Thus far, the Administration is not sure that the Asian Communists have accurately interpreted the warning signals from Washington. It is not sure that its allies in Europe appreciate the gravity of the United States commitment. And it is not sure that the American people understand the reasons for it.

Decision Publicized

Accordingly, the word is being passed with increasing vigor to the Congress, to the Washington press corps and to the Western allies.

These official assertions suggest that the decision to deny Southeast Asia to Communism was, in effect, taken a long time ago through circumstance and a cumulative series of lesser decisions.

The view that Laos can somehow be handled separately from South Vietnam has been abandoned. The earlier emphasis on limited involvement in South Vietnam's guerrilla war has been replaced by unlimited pledges of support for the whole region.

The hope here is that Hanoi and Peking are alert to this hardening of attitudes and that they have been properly forewarned by the less direct as well as public utterances of Administration leaders and, particularly, by the recent involvement of United States military planes in Laos.

Compromise Doubted

The subtleties of the situation have made the Administration reluctant to discuss future military moves beyond hints that every violation of past agreements in Southeast Asia and every change in the form of contest will draw a firm response.

All the comments here stress that the choice between war and peace lies in the hands of the Asian Communists and that Washington sees no way of negotiating a compromise. It will not sit down with Peking and Hanoi until recent violations for Laos are redressed because it could have no confidence in any new agreement.

To some extent, the Adminis-

Continued on Page 7, Column 1

JOHNSON IS FIRM

Vows in California to Oppose Violators of Freedom in World

By TOM WICKER
Special to The New York Times

SAN FRANCISCO, June 19—President Johnson promised tonight to open an "offensive in the pursuit of peace" based on an overwhelming military power that "makes it possible to seek agreement without fearing loss of liberty."

The President, addressing an audience of nearly 2,500 at a Democratic party fund-raising dinner, also pledged stern American opposition to "those who believe they can violate their neighbor's borders and steal their neighbor's freedom."

At the end of a day in California during which he gave several indications that he expected to be President for at least four more years, Mr. Johnson said he wanted to double the size of the Peace Corps, pursue what he called the "great society" with "the vision and valor of pioneers" and achieve "full equity for all our people."

Earlier in the day, before an enthusiastic welcome from more than 300,000 San Franciscans who lined Market Street to see his motorcade, the President came as near as he ever has to predicting his election in November.

Predicts the Good Life

"A Government which can get things done and knows where it is going," he said, "is the kind of Government you have had for the past four years—and that is the kind of Government you are going to get for the next four years."

Mr. Johnson's remarks were made at the dedication of a new Federal office building in downtown San Francisco. Before an audience he also spoke at Edwards Air Force Base in the Mojave Desert and broke ground for a new Oakland Bay area rapid transit system at ceremonies in Concord.

It was not until tonight, when he attended the $100-a-plate fund-raising dinner, that Mr. Johnson played an openly political role.

At every stop he voiced his prophecies of the good life for every American, promising Californians the lion's share.

At the party dinner, he shifted his emphasis somewhat, detailing the increases since 1960 in American military might. He added:

"We have used that strength not to intimidate others, but to

Continued on Page 6, Column 4

SENATOR KENNEDY HURT IN AIR CRASH; BAYH INJURED, TOO

Both Are in Fair Condition in Massachusetts Hospital —Pilot of Plane Killed

By The Associated Press

SOUTHAMPTON, Mass., Saturday, June 20—Senator Edward M. Kennedy, younger brother of President Kennedy and Senator Birch Bayh were injured in the crash of a private plane last night while on the way to the Massachusetts Democratic Convention.

The pilot was killed and two other persons were injured. Mr. Kennedy was semiconscious.

Both Senators were reported in fair condition at Cooley Dickinson Hospital in nearby Northampton.

Also injured were Mrs. Bayh, as reported in good condition, and Edward Moss of Andover, administrative aide to Mr. Ken-

Senator Edward M. Kennedy
Associated Press

nedy, who was reported in critical condition.

The pilot was identified as Edwin J. Zimny, 48 years old, of Lawrence, a last-minute substitute for the regular Kennedy pilot.

Senator Kennedy, Democrat of Massachusetts, was treated in an emergency room for back and chest injuries. His wife, Joan, visited him after he was transferred to an intensive-care unit.

Senator Bayh, Democrat of Indiana, suffered a hip injury. Mrs. Bayh was reported suffering from shock.

Mr. Kennedy's parents, Mr. and Mrs. Joseph P. Kennedy, were vacationing at their summer home in Hyannis Port, were not told of the plane crash.

Attorney General Robert F. Kennedy, brother of the Senator, boarded the family plane with an aide and was reported on the way to Boston.

Two Civil Aeronautics Board investigators were sent from

Continued on Page 54, Column 1

North Katanga City Is Seized By Rebels, the Congo Reports

Europeans Flee Albertville, Crossing Lake Tanganyika to Nearby Barundi

By J. ANTHONY LUKAS
Special to The New York Times

LEOPOLDVILLE, the Congo, June 19—Albertville, the capital of North Katanga Province, was reported today to have fallen to anti-Government rebels.

According to messages reaching here, rebels striking south along the shore of Lake Tanganyika entered the city about midday. It is not known here whether there was any resistance from Congolese soldiers there.

Many of the city's Europeans have fled in steamers across the lake. At least 150 women and children left on two steamers last night for Bujumbura, the capital of Burundi.

Another steamer, with 350 persons aboard, was scheduled to leave early this afternoon, but it was not whether it got away.

Meanwhile, the United States Embassy here said that two American civilian pilots who had been flying combat missions for the Congolese Army had voluntarily decided to cease flights. An embassy official said the pilots made their decision after they learned that they might be subject to penalties under United States law

Continued on Page 4, Column 3

PRESIDENT'S PLEA

He Declares the Task Now Is to Change Law Into Custom

Special to The New York Times

SAN FRANCISCO, June 19—President Johnson called the Senate passage of his civil rights bill today a "challenge to men of good will in every part of the country to transform the commands of our law into the customs of our land."

Mr. Johnson said it was now the nation's task "to reach beyond the content of the bill to conquer the barriers of poor education, poverty, and squalid housing which are an inheritance of past injustice and an impediment to future advance."

He said that he did not "underestimate the depth of the passions involved in the struggle for racial equality."

But he also spoke of "a large reservoir of goodwill and compassion, of decency and fair play which seeks a vision of justice without violence in the streets."

Johnson Statement

"Senate passage of the civil rights bill is a major step toward equal opportunities for all Americans. I congratulate Senators of both parties who worked to make passage possible.

"I look forward to the day, which will not be long forthcoming, when the bill becomes law. That will be a milestone in America's progress toward full justice for all her citizens.

"No single act of Congress can, by itself, eliminate discrimination and prejudice, hatred and injustice.

Broad National Consensus

"But this bill goes further to invest the rights of man with the protection of law than any legislation in this century.

"First, it will provide a carefully designed code to test and enforce the right of every American to go to school, to get a job, to vote, and to pursue his life unhampered by the barriers of racial discrimination.

"Second, it will, in itself, help educate all Americans to their responsibility to give equal treatment to their fellow citizens.

"Third, it will enlist one of the most powerful moral forces of American society on the side of civil rights—the moral obligation to respect and obey the law of the land.

"Fourth, and perhaps most important, this bill is a renewal and a re-enforcement, a symbol and a strengthening of that abiding commitment to human dignity and the equality of man which has been the guid-

Continued on Page 11, Column 6

CIVIL RIGHTS BILL PASSED, 73-27; JOHNSON URGES ALL TO COMPLY; DIRKSEN BERATES GOLDWATER

ON HAND FOR THE VOTE: Visitors waiting outside the Capitol yesterday for admittance to the Senate Chamber, before the vote on the civil rights bill was registered.
United Press International Telephoto

ARIZONAN TARGET OF G.O.P. LEADER

Illinoisan, in Speech on the Senate Floor, Scores View Bill Is Unconstitutional

By ANTHONY LEWIS
Special to The New York Times

WASHINGTON, June 19—The Republican leader in the Senate, Everett McKinley Dirksen of Illinois, closed the civil rights debate tonight with a biting attack on his party's leading Presidential prospect, Senator Barry Goldwater.

Senator Goldwater's announced opposition to the bill brought on the attack. He said yesterday that he could not "in good conscience" vote for the bill because he thought it was "unconstitutional" and would lead to a "police state."

Earlier, it was reported that former President Dwight D. Eisenhower had indicated to Mr. Goldwater that the general would not hold a negative view on the bill against the Arizonan.

On the floor of the Senate, Mr. Dirksen ridiculed the constitutional argument and moral position.

Looking often at Senator Goldwater, though never mentioning him by name, Mr. Dirksen in effect challenged the likely nominee of his party on what may be the chief issue at the Republican National Convention next month.

Dirksen Cites Legislation

First, Senator Dirksen mentioned many past pledges of legislation that had first been denounced as "unconstitutional." He listed the child labor prohibition, the Pure Food and Drug Act, the Minimum Wage Law and Social Security.

"It required no constitutional amendment," Senator Dirksen said, "to bring about all these forward thrusts in the interests of the people.

"It leads me to one conclusion: in the history of mankind, there is an inexorable moral force that moves us forward.

"No matter the resistance of people who do not fully understand, it will not be denied."

At this point, Senator Dirksen turned and looked directly at Senator Goldwater, who sat at his desk at the side of the chamber. Thrusting his right arm in Senator Goldwater's direction, he said:

"Utter all the extreme opin-

Continued on Page 11, Column 6

Rights Bill Roll-Call Vote

By The Associated Press

WASHINGTON, June 19—Following is the 73-27 vote by which the Senate passed the civil rights bill tonight:

FOR PASSAGE—73

Democrats—46

Anderson (N.M.)	Hayden (Ariz.)	Monroney (Okla.)
Bartlett (Alaska)	Hill (Ala.)	Morse (Ore.)
Bayh (Ind.)	Inouye (Hawaii)	Moss (Utah)
Brewster (Md.)	Jackson (Wash.)	Muskie (Me.)
Bible (Nev.)	Kennedy (Mass.)	Nelson (Wis.)
Burdick (N.D.)	Lausche (Ohio)	Neuberger (Ore.)
Cannon (Nev.)	Long (Mo.)	Pastore (R. I.)
Church (Idaho)	Magnuson (Wash.)	Pell (R. I.)
Clark (Pa.)	Mansfield (Mont.)	Proxmire (Wis.)
Dodd (Conn.)	McCarthy (Minn.)	Randolph (W.Va.)
Douglas (Ill.)	McGee (Wyo.)	Ribicoff (Conn.)
Edmondson (Okla.)	McGovern (S.D.)	Symington (Mo.)
Engle (Calif.)	McIntyre (N.H.)	Williams (N.J.)
Gruening (Alaska)	McNamara (Mich.)	Yarborough (Tex.)
Hart (Mich.)	Metcalf (Mont.)	Young (Ohio)
Hartke (Ind.)		

Republicans—27

Aiken (Vt.)	Dirksen (Ill.)	Morton (Ky.)
Allott (Colo.)	Dominick (Colo.)	Mundt (S. D.)
Beall (Md.)	Fong (Hawaii)	Pearson (Kan.)
Bennett (Utah)	Hruska (Neb.)	Prouty (Vt.)
Boggs (Del.)	Javits (N.Y.)	Saltonstall (Mass.)
Carlson (Kan.)	Jordan (Idaho)	Scott (Pa.)
Case (N. J.)	Keating (N. Y.)	Smith (Me.)
Cooper (Ky.)	Kuchel (Calif.)	Williams (Del.)
Curtis (Neb.)	Miller (Iowa)	Young (N. D.)

AGAINST PASSAGE—27

Democrats—21

Byrd (Va.)	Hill (Ala.)	Russell (Ga.)
Byrd (W. Va.)	Holland (Fla.)	Smathers (Fla.)
Eastland (Miss.)	Johnston (S. C.)	Sparkman (Ala.)
Ellender (La.)	Jordan (N. C.)	Stennis (Miss.)
Ervin (N. C.)	Long (La.)	Talmadge (Ga.)
Fulbright (Ark.)	McClellan (Ark.)	Thurmond (S. C.)
Gore (Tenn.)	Robertson (Va.)	Walters (Tenn.)
Cotton (N. H.)		

Republicans—6

Cotton (N. H.)	Hickenlooper (Iowa)	Simpson (Wyo.)
Goldwater (Ariz.)	Mechem (N.M.)	Tower (Tex.)

ACTION BY SENATE

Revised Measure Now Goes Back to House for Concurrence

By E. W. KENWORTHY
Special to The New York Times

WASHINGTON, June 19—The Senate passed the civil rights bill today by a vote of 73 to 27.

The final roll-call came at 7:40 P.M. on the 83d day of debate, nine days after closure was invoked.

Voting for the bill were 46 Democrats and 27 Republicans. Voting against it were 21 Democrats and six Republicans.

Except for Senator Robert C. Byrd of West Virginia, all the Democratic votes against the bill came from Southerners.

Senator Barry Goldwater of Arizona voted against the bill, as he said yesterday he would. The five other Republicans opposing it all support Mr. Goldwater's candidacy for the Republican Presidential nomination.

They were Bourke B. Hickenlooper of Iowa, chairman of the Senate Republican Policy Committee; Norris Cotton of New Hampshire, Edwin L. Mechem of New Mexico, Milward L. Simpson of Wyoming and John G. Tower of Texas.

2 Pledge Acceptance

The bill will now go back to the House for consideration of the changes that the Senate made in the measure the House passed last Feb. 10 by a vote of 290 to 130.

Tonight, Representatives Emanuel Celler, Democrat of New York, and William M. McCulloch, Republican of Ohio, who are the chairman and ranking minority member of the House Judiciary Committee, said that they would accept the Senate version of the bill.

"We believe that the House membership will take the same position," they said.

With the support of these two men, who were responsible for the House bill, acceptance of the Senate bill in the House is assured.

President Johnson hopes to have the bill on his desk by July 2 at the latest so that he can sign it on the Fourth of July.

Powers of the Bill

The bill passed by the Senate outlaws discrimination in places of public accommodation, publicly owned facilities, employment and union membership and Federally aided programs.

It gives the Attorney General new powers to speed school desegregation and enforce the Negro's right to vote.

The Senate bill differs from the House measure chiefly in giving states and local communities more scope and time to deal with complaints of discrimination in hiring and public accommodations. It allows the Attorney General to initiate suits in these areas where he finds a "pattern" of discrimination, but does not permit him, as did the House bill, to file suits on behalf of individuals.

After the roll-call, several thousand people gathered in the plaza before the floodlit Capitol to applaud the Senate Democratic leader, Mike Mansfield of Montana, and the Republican leader, Everett McKinley Dirksen of Illinois. Mr. Dirksen was instrumental in shaping the compromise that the Senate passed.

Burke Marshall, the Justice Department's civil rights chief, said after the bill was passed tonight that the department would move promptly to enforce the measure.

"I think there is going to be compliance with this bill," Mr. Marshall said. "That's the first step.

"But where there is a pattern

Continued on Page 10, Column 1

Erhard Bars Visit To the Soviet Union

Special to The New York Times

BONN, June 19—Chancellor Ludwig Erhard turned down today an unofficial but urgent Soviet invitation to go to Moscow for an attempt at improving Soviet-West German relations.

He suggested instead that the Soviet Premier ask for an official invitation to Bonn if he thought the trip would be worthwhile.

At his first news conference here in six months, Dr. Erhard carefully held open the door for an eventual encounter with Premier Khrushchev while dashing cold water on the prospects of settling soon any of the fundamental questions that divide Bonn and Moscow.

As he spoke, Bonn's Western allies were putting the final touches

Continued on Page 2, Column 4

Negro Leaders Hail Passage; Some Southerners Voice Anger

CORE Plans Tests

By MARTIN ARNOLD

Leaders of national civil rights groups last night hailed the Senate passage of the civil rights bill, and vowed that the measure would be quickly tested.

There was little indication that the Senate's action would reduce the number of demonstrations in the immediate future.

James L. Farmer, national director of the Congress of Racial Equality, said that CORE would press for implementation and enforcement of the bill's provisions.

Many Negroes approached on the streets in the South had little, if any comment.

Region's Reaction Varied

By United Press International

ATLANTA, June 19—Deep South politicians and newsmen lashed out angrily at passage of the civil rights bill, and an elderly Negro said, "I'll believe it when I see it."

Gov. George C. Wallace of Alabama declared that "this is a sad day for individual freedom and liberty," but a Chattanooga housewife said, "I firmly believe in it."

Reaction differed sharply between stanchly segregationist areas and areas where there has been desegregation.

"I think you just don't know much about it. I'm afraid to say," said a Negro in Nashville.

"It is good, I am glad," said George Thomson, a 40-year-old Negro cab driver in Montgomery, Ala.

Jefferson Johnson, an elderly Negro selling ice cream on a street in Birmingham, Ala., said:

"I'll believe it when I see it. I hope it'll do good, but—well

Continued on Page 12, Column 6

Yanks Woo Cabbies With 20,000 Tickets

By ROBERT LIPSYTE

The New York Yankees, long lordly and aloof atop baseball's corporate standings, have gone down to the street to wage promotional warfare.

They have given away free, to more than 10,000 reserved tickets worth $25,000 to more than 5,000 city cab drivers on the sidewalk along Broadway between 60th and 61st Streets in the last two days. Today, they expect to give away 10,000 more.

The Yankees' first mass giveaway program is the latest in a series of gimmicks to raise lagging attendance and combat the Mets at the box office.

"The idea," said Robert O. Fishel, the Yankees' public relations director, "is to make

Continued on Page 18, Column 2

President Lyndon B. Johnson shakes hands with Dr. King after signing the Civil Rights Act.

ing Rights Act to allow federal officials to register black people turned away by state officials.

By 1964, the nonviolent civil rights movement had begun to come apart. Three young civil rights workers, Andrew Goodman, Michael Schwerner, and James Chaney, were killed in Phil-adelphia, Mississippi. Their bodies, buried in an earthen dam, were not found for six weeks. White violence against SNCC workers in Alabama and Mississippi in the summer of 1964 caused SNCC to turn away from nonviolence as an effective tactic.

Black Power

Dr. King and Malcolm X share warm smiles and a friendly handshake after a meeting discussing the Civil Rights Bill.

Tired of seeing their young workers being beaten, and sometimes even killed, SNCC members voted in a new executive director, Stokely Carmichael, who insisted that it was time for new tactics. In 1966, Carmichael issued a call for "Black Power!"

The new black militancy could also be seen in the rise of the Black Panthers, a California-based organization that believed in self-defense and whose members openly carried guns.

And it could be seen in the growth of the Nation of Islam, sometimes called

Stokely Carmichael and H. Rap Brown, both of SNCC (Student Nonviolent Coordinating Committee), unite with students protesting discriminatory policies at New York City's Columbia University, April 26, 1968.

Armed with weapons, Bobby Seale, national chair of the Black Panther party, and defense minister Huey Newton, stand in front of party headquarters in Oakland, California, 1969.

Henry McIntyre of New York's Black Panther party talks to a child attending one of the party's liberation schools in Brooklyn.

the Black Muslims, a group based in Chicago that preached black nationalism and separatism. Its most famous minister, Malcolm X, helped increase its membership with his fiery oratory about black pride and self-help. The Black Muslims lost much of their momentum when Malcolm X left the Nation of Islam to form his own organization. Four Muslims assassinated him in 1965.

On from Selma

The rise in militancy troubled Dr. King, who still believed that nonviolence was the best tactic. In 1964 he was awarded the Nobel Peace Prize for his continuing commitment to peaceful solutions to race problems. The following year, he led a series of nonviolent demonstrations for the right to vote in Selma, Alabama. In March 1965, these demonstrations culminated in a huge march, with federal protection, from Selma to Montgomery, the capital of Alabama.

As his parents and wife look on, Dr. King is congratulated by Prince Harald and King Olav of Norway after receiving the Nobel Peace Prize, December 10, 1964.

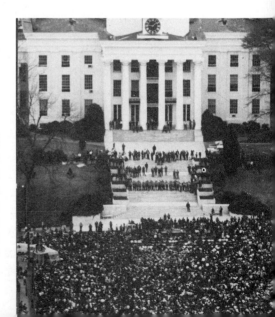

Thirty thousand civil rights demonstrators surround the Alabama State Capitol Dome in Montgomery at the finale of the Selma to Montgomery march.

Civil rights activists demonstrate for voting rights in the South during the march from Selma to Montgomery, Alabama, March 1965.

A scuffle breaks out as police charge into a group of civil rights activists during the march from Selma to Montgomery.

A white woman from Detroit named Viola Liuzzo, who had volunteered to drive marchers back and forth, was killed by four Ku Klux Klansmen.

In August 1965, Watts, the black section of Los Angeles, exploded in the worst riots in the nation's history. Civil rights leaders like Dr. King realized that while concentrating on making legal gains in the South, the civil rights movement had done little to improve the lives of black people in other areas of the country. While there was no outright segregation in these areas, there was much discrimination. Black people there suffered in ghettos, with poor schools and severe unemployment.

The following year, King and the

SCLC took the movement to Chicago, demanding an end to discrimination in housing, schools, and employment. But because these conditions were not a result of legalized segregation, King found them hard to attack with the same tactics of marches and demonstrations that he had used in the South. The momentum of the civil rights movement had stalled and King and other, older civil rights leaders were being called has-beens by the younger, more militant leaders.

James Meredith, the first black to gain admission to the University of Mississippi, after being shot in Jackson, Mississippi, June 1966.

A young man is pulled from the debris of a looted storefront in the aftermath of the Watts Riots, August 12, 1965.

An army medic pleads for help during the battle of Chu Pong, South Vietnam, as he assists a wounded soldier, November 2, 1972.

Still, King's voice was powerful, and his opinions could influence many people. He used this influence to speak out against the Vietnam War, although he angered many people by doing so.

King kept on participating in marches and protests that were like the ones that had been so successful in the South. Until that last moment on April 4, 1968, at the Lorraine Motel, he believed in nonviolent protest.

Blacks in Office

Martin Luther King, Jr.'s, stress on black voting rights began to pay off very soon after he died. The first major gains were in northern cities. In the fall of 1967, Carl Stokes of Cleveland, Ohio, and Richard Gordon Hatcher of Gary, Indiana, became the first black mayors of major urban centers. In 1970, Kenneth Gibson of Newark, New Jersey, became the first black mayor of a major city on the eastern seaboard.

In 1973, Thomas Bradley was elected mayor of Los Angeles, California, where the majority of the voters were white. And finally, in 1989, New York City, the most populous city in the United States, elected David N. Dinkins its first black mayor.

David Dinkins, the first African American mayor of New York City is sworn into office as his wife Joyce, and Governor Mario Cuomo watch.

While these black political victories occurred in areas where blacks had long enjoyed the right to vote, they can still be traced to the civil rights movement. Before that time, the black vote was largely unorganized. Now northern black leaders realized they could organize black

Carl Stokes of Cleveland, Ohio, the first elected black mayor of a major United States city.

voters, and once they did, blacks were elected to high political offices.

It did not take long after Dr. King's death for blacks in the South to make their political clout felt. In 1969 James Charles Evers became mayor of Fayette, Mississippi, the first time since Reconstruction that a black mayor was elected in a southern town with white residents. Over the next twenty years blacks in the South used their numbers and their new voting power to gain a great deal of political power. Atlanta,

Tom Bradley takes the oath of office as mayor of Los Angeles, July 1, 1973.

Navy Lieutenant Robert O. Goodman clasps hands with Reverend Jesse Jackson after Jackson successfully negotiated Goodman's release from Syria.

Georgia, the largest city in the South, elected two black mayors in a row, Maynard Jackson and Andrew Young. In 1989, the southern state of Virginia became the first state to elect a black governor, L. Douglas Wilder.

In 1984 and 1988, Jesse Jackson, born in South Carolina, who had been one of Dr. King's aides at the time of his assassination, campaigned for the Democratic presidential nomination. Although he did not win, he became a voice to be reckoned with in the Democratic Party.

Dr. King had lived to see some of the most insulting aspects of segregation ended—the "Colored" and "White" signs at southern restrooms and water fountains, the separate seating on public buses, the whites-only restaurants and libraries and school buses. Had he lived longer, he would have seen even more signs of hope—black children and white children going to school together, black people in professions that were once closed to them, the rise of a solid black middle class.

Governor Lawrence Douglas Wilder of Virginia, the first elected African American governor in the history of the United States.

Many of these changes were due to Supreme Court rulings. During the 1960s and 1970s, the high court heard many cases on school desegregation, for although it had ruled that segregated schools were unconstitutional in 1955, it took a long time for schools to be integrated. Thurgood Marshall, the first and, to date, the only black Associate Justice, joined with liberal members of the court to rule against communities that dragged their feet on integration.

Congresswoman Barbara Jordan of Texas addresses a House judiciary subcommittee.

Shirley Chisholm of Brooklyn, New York, gives the victory sign after becoming the first black female member of Congress.

The late mayor Harold Washington of Chicago exchanges greetings with Reverend Jesse Jackson at a press conference.

Many of the gains made by blacks since the death of Dr. King have come about as a result of "affirmative action." President Lyndon Johnson used the term, which was actually coined by James Farmer, to mean giving every opportunity possible to blacks because of the centuries of discrimination they had suffered. Many colleges and universities, government agencies, and some private businesses, made a special effort to recruit qualified blacks.

The courts ruled in 1978 that racial quotas—a specific number or percent-age of places for blacks—were unconstitutional. It also ruled that race could be considered as one of many factors in admitting students.

During the 1980s, President Reagan appointed justices to the Supreme Court who were more conservative in their interpretation of the Constitution.

Not just the Supreme Court, but the nation as a whole seemed to become more conservative in its views on race than previously. In October 1990, President George Bush vetoed a Civil Rights Act.

The Struggle Goes On

Had he lived, Dr. King would have seen that there was still a great deal yet to be done. The legacy of slavery and second-class citizenship still exists and prevents millions of black people from enjoying equality of opportunity. While a solid black middle class has emerged since the civil rights movement, there is a huge black underclass. Drugs and crime, lack of education, unemploy-

The color line is a thing of the past for two soldiers being served in a drugstore in San Antonio, Texas.

In Springfield, Massachusetts, smiles abound from the faces of elementary school students, where busing proceeded without incident.

Students from Charlotte, North Carolina, and Boston, Massachusetts, gather at a forum to discuss school desegregation plans in their cities.

ment, and homelessness affect this class in greater proportion than it does poor whites. These problems are not as easily addressed by major legislation as the problems suffered by southern blacks before the civil rights movement. In fact, there has been no major civil rights legislation since the 1960s. And even now changes in the law do not automatically bring about changes in people's hearts and minds. Dr. Martin Luther King, Jr.'s, dream has yet to be fulfilled.

Still, the gains made by African Americans (and the changes in the hearts of white Americans) are proof that nonviolent demonstrations to fight for rights work.

The effect of the civil rights movement has also been felt beyond American shores. Black South Africans and others around the world who still have little freedom point to the civil rights movement as evidence that nonviolent protest can be effective. America can be proud of that.

Americans can be proud, too, that a federal holiday honoring the birthday of Dr. King is now observed. No other individual, black or white, who was not a president of the United States is so honored. Every year, on the Monday closest to January 15, Dr. King's birthday, Americans pause to honor this courageous man.

Black soldiers and an army nurse serving in Vietnam take time out to observe the birthday of Dr. King.

Important Dates in the Fight for African American Rights

1663

September 13 — First serious slave conspiracy in colonial America in Gloucester County, Virginia

1712

April 7 — Slave revolt in New York

1739

September 9 — Slave revolt in Stono, South Carolina

1770

March 5 — Crispus Attucks, the first black, and one of the first five people, killed in Revolutionary cause

1775

April 14 — First abolition society in the United States organized in Philadelphia, Pennsylvania

First black Baptist Church is founded by David George, a runaway slave

1776

January 16 — Continental Congress approves General George Washington's order to enlist free Negroes

1777

July 2 — Vermont is the first American state to abolish slavery

1781

James Forten, a black crewman on the privateer *Royal Louis* is taken prisoner

1787

September 12 — Prince Hall receives a charter from the Grand Lodge of England for the first Negro Masonic lodge in America

Richard Allen and Absalom Jones found the Free African Society

1794

Richard Allen organizes Bethel African Methodist Episcopal Church in Philadelphia

1796

Zion Methodist Church organized in New York City

1800

In New York, Peter Williams and James Varick form their own Zion church

1820

March 3 — Missouri Compromise enacted, banning slavery to the north of southern boundary of Missouri

1822

May 30 — Denmark Vesey's conspiracy uncovered; Vesey and others hanged on July 2

1827

March 16 — *Freedom's Journal,* first black newspaper, published in New York City by John B. Russwurm

1829

September 28 — David Walker publishes *Walker's Appeal* in Boston

1830

September 20 — First national black convention meets at Philadelphia's Bethel Church, presided over by Richard Allen

1831

January 1 — William Lloyd Garrison publishes the abolitionist newspaper, *Liberator*

August 21–22 — Nat Turner revolt, Southampton County, Virginia; Turner is hanged in November

1839

Joseph Cinque leads a slave revolt aboard the *Amistad.* Atlantic slave trade outlawed in the United States

1843

June 1 — Sojourner Truth begins her work as an abolitionist

1847

December 3 — Frederick Douglass publishes the first issue of his newspaper, *North Star*

1849

Harriet Tubman escapes from slavery in Maryland; will return to the South nineteen times to help other slaves escape

1854

May 30—Kansas-Nebraska Act repeals Missouri Compromise and opens the Northern Territory to slavery

1857

March 6—Dred Scott decision by U.S. Supreme Court opens federal territory to slavery and denies citizenship to American blacks

1859

October 16–17—John Brown attacks U.S. arsenal at Harpers Ferry, Virginia. Brown is hanged on December 2

1861

April 12—Confederates attack Fort Sumter; Civil War begins

1862

May 13—Robert Smalls sails the armed Confederate steamer *Planter* out of Charleston Harbor and presents it to the U.S. Navy

July 17—Congress authorizes President Lincoln to accept blacks for military service

1863

January 1—President Lincoln signs the Emancipation Proclamation freeing the slaves in all rebel states

January 26—War Department authorizes Massachusetts governor to recruit the first black troops, the Fifty-fourth Massachusetts Volunteers, which makes its famous charge on Fort Wagner on July 18

July 13–17—New York City Draft Riots by white workers who blame blacks for the Civil War

1865

January 11—Confederate General Robert E. Lee recommends arming the slaves

January 31—Congress passes the Thirteenth Amendment abolishing slavery; it becomes part of the Constitution December 18

March 3—Congress establishes the Freedmen's Bureau to aid refugees and freedmen

April 9—General Robert E. Lee surrenders

April 15—President Lincoln assassinated

1866

April 9—Civil Rights Bill passed over President Johnson's veto

1867

March 2—Congress passes first Reconstruction Acts

April—First meeting of Ku Klux Klan in Nashville, Tennessee

1868

January 14—Constitutional convention meets in Charleston, South Carolina, with a majority of black delegates

June 13—Ex-slave Oscar Dunn becomes lieutenant governor of Louisiana

July 28—Fourteenth Amendment becomes part of the Constitution; declares all persons born or naturalized in the United States are citizens and entitled to the equal protection of its laws

1870

March 30—Fifteenth Amendment becomes part of the Constitution; declares that the right to vote cannot be denied because of race or previous condition of servitude

December 12—Joseph H. Rainey of South Carolina sworn in as first black in the U.S. House of Representatives

1872

December 11—P.B.S. Pinchback, mulatto, sworn in as acting governor of Louisiana; elected to the U.S. Senate the following year

1875

March 1—Civil Rights Bill enacted by Congress; gives blacks the right to equal treatment in public places and transport

1877

President Rutherford B. Hayes orders federal troops to leave the South

1879

In "Exodus of 1879," southern blacks flee political and economic exploitation

1881

Booker T. Washington founds Tuskegee Institute

1883

November 26—U.S. Supreme Court declares 1875 Civil Rights Act unconstitutional

1887

Beginning of Jim Crow laws

1890

August 12–November 1—Mississippi constitutional convention begins systematic exclusion of blacks from politics

1895

September 18—Booker T. Washington delivers "Atlanta Compromise" address

1896

May 18—U.S. Supreme Court in *Plessy v. Ferguson* case upholds the doctrine of "separate but equal"

1898

Blacks fight in Spanish-American War

1909

February 12—National Association for the Advancement of Colored People (NAACP) founded by W.E.B. Du Bois and other influential blacks and whites; organization is incorporated in 1910

1910

National Urban League founded

1917

April 6—America enters World War I

1920

August 1—National convention of Marcus Garvey's Universal Negro Improvement Association opens in Harlem, New York City

1927

December—Marcus Garvey deported as an undesirable alien

1929

October—Stock Market Crash

1931

April 6—First of the "Scottsboro Boys" trials begins

1936

December 8—NAACP files first suit in campaign for equal pay for black teachers

Mary McLeod Bethune, founder and president of Bethune-Cookman College, named director of the Division of Negro Affairs of the National Youth Administration

1937

Adam Clayton Powell, Jr., becomes minister of Abyssinian Baptist Church

1941

January 16—War Department announces the formation of the first Army Air Corps squadron for black cadets

April 18—Bus companies in New York City agree to hire black drivers and mechanics after a four-week boycott led by the Reverend Adam Clayton Powell, Jr.

June 18—A. Philip Randolph and others meet with President Roosevelt about their proposed March on Washington on July 1 to protest discrimination in war industries

June 25—President Roosevelt signs Executive Order 8802 forbidding discrimination in war industries; Randolph calls off the march

First U.S. Army flying school for black cadets dedicated at Tuskegee Institute, Alabama

December 7—Japanese bomb U.S. naval base at Pearl Harbor, Hawaii

1942

Congress of Racial Equality (CORE) founded by James Farmer

1944

August 1—Adam Clayton Powell, Jr., elected the first black congressman from the East

1945

August 14—World War II ends

1946

June 3—U.S. Supreme Court bans segregation on interstate buses

December 5—President Truman creates Committee on Civil Rights

1947

April 9—Congress of Racial Equality (CORE) sends first "Freedom Rider" group to test the Supreme Court ban on segregation in interstate travel

1948

July 26—President Truman issues Executive Order 9981 directing equality of opportunity in the armed forces

1951

NAACP begins attack on ''separate but equal'' education

1954

May 17 — U.S. Supreme Court in *Brown v. Topeka Board of Education* rules that racial segregation in public schools is unconstitutional

1955

December 1 — Rosa Parks is arrested in Montgomery, Alabama, for not giving up her bus seat to a white person; the Montgomery Bus Boycott begins December 5

1956

November 13 — U.S. Supreme Court upholds a lower court decision banning segregation on Montgomery, Alabama, city buses; Martin Luther King, Jr., and other boycott leaders call off the boycott a month later

1957

February 14 — Southern Christian Leadership Conference (SCLC) organized, with Dr. Martin Luther King, Jr., as president

August 29 — Congress passes first Civil Rights Act since Reconstruction

September 24 — President Eisenhower orders federal troops to Little Rock, Arkansas, to prevent interference with school integration

1960

February 1 — Students from North Carolina A&T sit in at a ''whites only'' Woolworth's lunch counter; by February 10 the movement has spread to five other southern cities

April 15–17 — Student Nonviolent Coordinating Committee (SNCC) organized

May 6 — President Eisenhower signs Civil Rights Act of 1960

1961

May 4 — CORE launches a series of Freedom Rides into the South

1963

April 3 — Dr. Martin Luther King, Jr., opens anti-segregation campaign in Birmingham, Alabama

June 12 — Medgar Evers shot in Mississippi

August 28 — More than 250,000 persons participate in March on Washington organized by Bayard Rustin

September 15 — Sixteenth Street Baptist Church in Birmingham, Alabama, is bombed; four young girls are killed

November 22 — President Kennedy assassinated in Dallas, Texas

1964

June 21 — Andrew Goodman and Michael Schwerner from New York City, and James Chaney from Meridian, Mississippi, working on a SNCC voting rights project, are murdered; members of the Ku Klux Klan are convicted for the first time

July 2 — Civil Rights Act signed by President Johnson

Dr. Martin Luther King, Jr., wins the Nobel Peace Prize

1965

February 21 — Malcolm X murdered

March 21–25 — Selma-to-Montgomery March

March 25 — Mrs. Viola Liuzzo killed by Ku Klux Klan members

August 11–16 — Blacks in Watts section of Los Angeles riot

August 4 — President Johnson signs Voting Rights Bill

1966

June — Stokely Carmichael, head of SNCC, issues his call for ''Black Power''

August 5 — Dr. Martin Luther King, Jr., stoned as he leads a march through Chicago's South Side

1967

March 25 — King attacks U.S. policy in Vietnam at Chicago march

June 13 — Thurgood Marshall, former NAACP lawyer, nominated as Associate Justice of the U.S. Supreme Court; confirmed by Senate August 30

July 20–23 — Black Power conference in Newark, New Jersey, attracts largest and most diverse group of black American leaders ever assembled

1968

March 4 — Dr. King announces he will lead a Poor People's March on Washington in April

March 28 — Dr. King leads a protest march in support of striking sanitation workers in Memphis, Tennessee

April 4 — Dr. King assassinated by James Earl Ray in Memphis

April 11 — President Johnson signs a Civil Rights Bill banning discrimination in housing and making it a crime to interfere with civil rights workers

May 2 — Ralph David Abernathy, King's successor as head of the SCLC, leads Poor People's Campaign to Washington, D.C.

June 8 — James Earl Ray, Dr. Martin Luther King, Jr.'s, murderer is caught

November 7 — Carl Stokes of Cleveland, Ohio, and Richard Hatcher of Gary, Indiana, are first blacks to be elected mayors of major American cities

1969

James Charles Evers becomes mayor of Fayette, Mississippi

1970

June 16 — Kenneth Gibson elected first black mayor of Newark, New Jersey

1971

April 20 — U.S. Supreme Court rules in *Swann v. Charlotte-Mecklenburg* that busing to achieve integration in public schools is constitutional

1977

January 31 — Andrew J. Young, first black American ambassador to the United Nations, presents his credentials to U.N. Secretary General Kurt Waldheim

1978

June 28 — In the *Bakke* case, Supreme Court rules that affirmative action with strict racial quotas is illegal

1984

Jesse Jackson seeks the Democratic presidential nomination

1986

January 15 — Martin Luther King, Jr.'s, birthday celebrated as a federal holiday for the first time

1988

Jesse Jackson seeks the Democratic presidential nomination

1989

November 7 — L. Douglas Wilder of Virginia becomes the first black governor since Reconstruction; David N. Dinkins becomes the first black mayor of New York City

1990

October — President George Bush vetoes Civil Rights Act

1991

June 27 — Justice Thurgood Marshall announces his resignation from the Supreme Court

June 30 — National Civil Rights Museum opens at the Lorraine Motel

For Further Reading

Young Readers

Adler, David A. *A Picture Book of Martin Luther King, Jr.* New York: Holiday House, 1989

Davidson, Margaret. *I Have a Dream: The Story of Martin Luther King.* New York: Scholastic, 1986

Davis, Burke. *Black Heroes of the American Revolution.* New York: Harcourt, 1976

Faber, Doris and Harold. *The Assassination of Martin Luther King, Jr.* New York: Watts, 1978

Johnson Publishing Co., Inc. *Martin Luther King, Jr., 1929–1960: A Picture Biography.* Chicago, 1968

Kosof, Anna. *The Civil Rights Movement and its Legacy.* New York: Watts, 1989

McKissack, Patricia and Fredrick. *Martin Luther King, Jr.: Man of Peace.* Hillside, NJ: Enslow, 1991

Patrick, Diane. *Martin Luther King, Jr.* New York: Watts, 1990

Young-Adult Readers

Bernard, Jacqueline. *Journey Toward Freedom: The Story of Sojourner Truth.* New York: Norton, 1967

Darby, Jean. *Martin Luther King, Jr.* Minneapolis: Lerner, 1990

Harris, Jacqueline L. *Martin Luther King, Jr.* New York: Watts, 1983

Haskins, James. *The Life and Death of Martin Luther King, Jr.* New York: Lothrop, 1977

Katz, William Loren. *Breaking the Chains: African-American Slave Resistance.* New York: Atheneum, 1990.

McKissack, Patricia and Fredrick. *The Civil Rights Movement in America from 1865 to the Present.* Chicago: Children's Press, 1987

Meltzer, Milton. *The Black Americans: A History in their own Words.* New York: Crowell, 1984

Patterson, Lillie. *Martin Luther King, Jr., and the Freedom Movement.* New York: Facts on File, 1989

Tate, Eleanora E. *Thank You, Dr. Martin Luther King, Jr!* New York: Watts, 1990

Index   *Page references in italics indicate material in illustrations or photographs.*

speech, 72; Nobel Peace Prize awarded to, 78, *78*; nonviolent protest movement and, 66, 67, *67*, 71, 78, 79, 80, 81; voting rights and, 82
Korean War, *58*, 59
Ku Klux Klan, *36*, 37; lynchings and, 48; murders by, 79

L
Labor movement, 54
Language, Pidgin English, 14
Lee, Robert E., 25, 33, *33*
Lewis, John, *69*
Liberator (newspaper), 20, *21*
Lincoln, Abraham, *28*, 29, 31, *33*, 34, *34*, 35, *35*
Little Rock, Arkansas, 63, *63*, *64*, *65*
Liuzzo, Viola, 79
Lynchings: increases in, 50; newspaper reports of, 48, *48*, 49; New York City draft riots and, *32*; Reconstruction and, 39

M
Malcolm X, *76*, 77
Malloy, S.A., *55*
March on Washington (1963), *54*, 72
Marshall, Thurgood, 61, *61*, 83
Masonic Order, 19, *19*
McIntyre, Henry, *77*
Meredith, James, *80*
Migrations, of African Americans, 40, *41*, *42*, 44, *44*
Montgomery, Alabama, violence in, *69*
Montgomery (Alabama) Improvement Association, 66
Mothershed, Thelma, *64*
Music, 11–12, 14–15

N
Nabrit, James M., *61*
Nast, Thomas, *36*
National Association for the Advancement of Colored People (NAACP), 66; court battles fought by, 55; founding of, 47; integration activities of, 69, 71; Scottsboro (Alabama) Nine and, 52; separate but equal doctrine challenged by, 60–61
National Association of Colored Women, *43*
National Urban League, 47
Nation of Islam, 76–77
New Deal, 55
Newspapers, 48, 49
Newton, Huey, *77*
New York City, New York: draft riots (1863) in, *32*; Harlem Renaissance, 47, 50, *51*; race relations and, *48*; segregation in, 53
Nobel Peace Prize, King, Martin Luther, Jr. awarded, 78, *78*
Nonviolent protest movement: civil rights and, 66, *66*, 67, *67*; effectiveness of, 87; King, Martin Luther, Jr. and, 78, 79, 80, 81; white violence and, *72*, *73*, 75, *79*
North Carolina Agricultural and Technical College, 68, *68*
North Star (newspaper), 23

O
Olav (King of Norway), *78*

P
Parks, Rosa, 66, *66*
Pattillo, Melba, *64*
Philadelphia, Pennsylvania, race relations in, *43*
Pickett, Bill, *41*
Pidgin English, 14
Pinchback, Pinckney Benton Stewart, 37
Plessy, Homer, 43
Plessy v. Ferguson, 43
Politics: African American victories in, 82, *82*, 83, *83*, *84*, *85*; Reconstruction and, 34–39, 82
Powell, Adam Clayton, Jr., 52, 53, *53*, 54
Press. *See* Newspapers

Q
Quotas. *See* Racial quotas

R
Race riots: East St. Louis race riot, *48*; New York City draft riots (1863), *32*; Reconstruction and, 39; Watts (Los Angeles, California), 79, *80*; World War I and, 50
Racial quotas, courts and, 85
Randolph, A. Philip, 54, *54*, 56–57, 67, 72
Ray, Gloria, *64*
Ray, James Earl, 9, *9*
Reagan, Ronald, 85
Reconstruction, 34–39, 82
Religion: abolitionist movement and, 23; African American church, 18, *18*, 19, *19*; slaves and, 15
Republican Party, 35
Riots. *See* Race riots
Roberts, Terrance, *64*
Roosevelt, Franklin D., 55, 56–57, 59
Russwurm, John B., 20, *20*
Rustin, Bayard, 57, *59*, 72

S
Schwerner, Michael, *72*, 75
Scottsboro (Alabama) Nine, 52, *52*
Seale, Bobby, *77*
Segregation. *See also* Civil rights; Discrimination; Integration: African American migrations and, 44; armed forces and, 50; court battles against, 55; Jim Crow laws and, 40–41, 43; nonviolent protest movement and, 66, *66*; North and, 53; Reconstruction and, 37; United States Supreme Court and, 66, 69, 71
Selma (Alabama) march of 1965, 78, *78*, 79, *79*
Separate but equal doctrine: National Association for the Advancement of Colored People (NAACP) challenges, 60–61; Supreme Court declares, 43
Shaw, Robert Gould, *30*
Sit-ins, 59, 68, *68*, 69, *69*, 70, *70*, 71, *71*
Slave revolts, 12, *12*, 13, *13*
Slavery: *abolition of*; in North, 23; in South, 39; American Revolution and, 17; Civil War (U.S.) and, 29; legacy of, 86; *resistance to*; Civil War (U.S.), 29; Middle Passage, 10, 11, 12, *12*, 13,